Another Look at FAITH

Kenneth W. Hagin

Unless otherwise indicated, all Scripture quotations are taken from the *King James Version* of the Bible.

19 18 17 16 15 14 13   12 11 10 09 08 07 06

Another Look at Faith
ISBN-13: 978-0-89276-733-5
ISBN-10: 0-89276-733-2

In the U.S. write:
Kenneth Hagin Ministries
P.O. Box 50126
Tulsa, OK 74150-0126
1-888-28-FAITH
www.rhema.org

In Canada write:
Kenneth Hagin Ministries of Canada
P.O. Box 335, Station D
Etobicoke (Toronto), Ontario
Canada M9A 4X3
1-866-70-RHEMA
www.rhemacanada.org

Contents

Chapter 1
What Faith Is Not

And Jesus answering saith unto them, Have faith in God.

For verily I say unto you, That whosoever shall SAY unto this mountain, Be thou removed, and be thou cast into the sea; and shall not doubt in his heart, but shall believe that those things which he SAITH shall come to pass; he shall have whatsoever he SAITH.

Therefore I say unto you, What things soever ye desire, when ye pray, BELIEVE that ye receive them, and ye shall have them.

—Mark 11:22–24

Now faith is the substance of things hoped for, the evidence of things not seen.

—Hebrews 11:1

Jesus told us to have faith in God. The margin note in my *King James Bible* says, "Have the faith of God." God wants us to have *His* kind of faith. The God-kind of faith *believes* and *speaks*. That's how God created the universe in the first place (*see* Genesis chapter 1).

We need to take another look at faith—Bible faith—so we can understand the God-kind of faith. Some people say things about faith that don't line up with the Word of God. Many people have assumed things about faith that are not biblically correct. When people don't understand Bible faith, they often make false assumptions about it.

Their false ideas about faith influence their remarks, attitudes, and actions. What they assume to be faith is not biblical faith at all, so they end up disappointed, thinking that faith in God doesn't work. They are misled just because they don't know what Bible faith *is* and what it is *not*. So we need to take another look at faith and see what Bible faith really is.

One Misconception

For example, one misconception about faith is that it is wrong to believe God for specific things or for specific needs to be met. Some people say that we only need a general faith in God because believing God for a specific prayer request is manipulating Him, and that detracts from His sovereignty.

They teach that it is only appropriate to pray, "Lord, Thy will be done," because *we* can never know the will of God. Therefore, to pray for anything specific may be praying against the will of God.

For example, these people teach that you may be praying for God to meet a financial need in your life, while God may want you to be poor. So they believe God may want to teach you something by allowing you to suffer with lack and poverty. Therefore, they say that if you pray for God to meet your financial needs, you could be praying against the will of God.

According to this teaching, you can never pray about anything specific with any confidence. You can only pray, "Lord, Your will be done." And you can never know what God's will is because "God moves in mysterious ways, His wonders to perform."

But one problem with this teaching is that people assume that whatever the outcome, it must be God's will!

We *can* pray about our specific needs. The Bible teaches us that God *wants* to supply our specific needs.

> **PHILIPPIANS 4:19**
> **19 But my God shall supply all your need according to his riches in glory by Christ Jesus.**

God wants to meet our specific needs! In fact, you should be specific with God based on the promises in His Word. Faith begins where the will of God is known, and if you know what His Word promises, then you know you can receive your specific petition. This is what the *Bible* teaches!

> **1 JOHN 5:14,15**
> **14 And this is the confidence that we have in him, that, if we ask any thing according to his will, he heareth us:**
> **15 And if we know that he hear us, whatsoever we ask, we know that we have the petitions that we desired of him.**

How can believing God for specific requests be unscriptural? After all, if you don't believe God specifically for salvation, you can't get saved. Without faith to receive the baptism in the Holy Spirit, you can't receive this gift from God. Without faith, you can't receive any of the promises of God in your life.

Does the Bible give us any instances of people believing God for specific needs, such as healing? If people in the Bible believed God for specific needs to be met, then we can know it is scriptural to use our faith to receive specific petitions from God.

The Woman With the Issue of Blood

In Mark 5, there was a woman who had suffered for twelve years with an issue of blood. She needed to be healed. She had suffered many things of many physicians and was not better, but rather grew worse.

MARK 5:25–34
25 And a certain woman, which had an issue of blood twelve years,
26 And had suffered many things of many physicians, and had spent all that she had, and was nothing bettered, but rather grew worse,
27 When she had heard of Jesus, came in the press behind, and touched his garment.
28 For she said, If I may touch but his clothes, I shall be whole.
29 And straightway the fountain of her blood was dried up; and she felt in her body that she was healed of that plague.
30 And Jesus, immediately knowing in himself

> that virtue had gone out of him, turned him about
> in the press, and said, Who touched my clothes?
> 31 And his disciples said unto him, Thou seest the
> multitude thronging thee, and sayest thou, Who
> touched me?
> 32 And he looked round about to see her that had
> done this thing.
> 33 But the woman fearing and trembling, know-
> ing what was done in her, came and fell down
> before him, and told him all the truth.
> 34 And he said unto her, Daughter, thy faith hath
> made thee whole; go in peace, and be whole of thy
> plague.

The woman with the issue of blood said, "If I may touch but his clothes, I will be whole" (v. 28). In other words, she was believing God specifically for her healing. She had faith for a specific need to be met in her life—the healing of her body.

This woman believed that touching Jesus would heal her of a long-standing infirmity. She specifically believed she would be healed of the issue of blood she'd suffered with for twelve long years.

Notice that when Jesus asked, "Who touched Me?" He did not try to correct her theology or try to change the way she'd used her faith (v. 30). He did not go off on a doctrinal dissertation, telling her, "Don't ask Me to meet your *specific* needs or desires; I only answer *general* prayers."

Jesus simply looked at her and said, "Daughter, thy faith hath made thee whole" (v. 34). Her faith for a specific need was rewarded because she was healed and made completely whole!

The Lame Man at Lystra

Are there other instances in the Bible of people receiving specific needs met? Yes, remember the lame man who needed a specific healing in his feet and ankle bones?

Paul had preached in Lystra, and there was a crippled man in that city who needed to be healed. The man needed to be able to walk!

> **ACTS 14:8–10**
> **8 And there sat a certain man at Lystra, impotent in his feet, being a cripple from his mother's womb, who never had walked:**
> **9 The same heard Paul speak: who stedfastly beholding him, and perceiving that he had faith to be healed,**
> **10 Said with a loud voice, Stand upright on thy feet. And he leaped and walked.**

Not only did this man need to be healed, but Paul perceived that he had faith to be healed. However, if this man had never believed God to meet his specific need for healing, he never would have walked! He had faith for a specific need to be met—the healing of his feet and ankle bones.

My dad, Rev. Kenneth E. Hagin, had specific faith to be healed of a deformed heart and an incurable blood disease. I would not have been born if it hadn't been for my dad's faith in God's Word. I thank God today that my dad had faith to believe God for a specific need—the healing of an incurable disease!

You may remember from reading my dad's books and hearing him minister that as a teenager on his deathbed, a minister was asked to visit him so my dad could ask him about Mark 11:23 and 24.

The doctor had already told Dad that he only had a few days to live. Because of his condition, Dad couldn't really speak. So when the minister came, Dad tried to ask him if Mark 11:23 and 24 really meant what it said.

The minister couldn't understand what Dad was trying to say. So he just patted him on the head, and putting on his best professional voice, he said, "There, there, my boy. Just a few more days, and it will all be over."

But, thank God, a teenaged boy had faith in the Word of God! No one told him about faith or divine healing. He had never heard anyone preach about believing God's Word. He simply read the Word of God for himself and believed it.

This ministry has taught faith in God's Word because God gave Brother Hagin a special assignment or a special commission to teach faith. God told him, "Go teach My people faith."

This doesn't mean there's not more to the Word of God than faith or that faith is more important than other biblical doctrines. But faith is important because the Bible says, "Without faith it is impossible to please God" (Heb. 11:6).

The Bible also says, *"Now the just shall live by faith . . ."* (Heb. 10:38). Therefore, we emphasize faith and believing what the Word of God says about faith.

Faith Defined Biblically

The Bible defines faith for us in Hebrews chapter 11. And we can understand more about faith by looking at different translations of Hebrews 11:1 that help define what faith is.

(King James Version)

Now faith is the substance of things hoped for, the evidence of things not seen.

(New International Version)

Now faith is being sure of what we hope for and certain of what we do not see.

(American Standard Version)

Now faith is assurance of things hoped for, a conviction of things not seen.

(Weymouth)

Now faith is a confident assurance of that for which we hope, a conviction of the reality of things which we do not see.

(Goodspeed)

Faith means the assurance of what we hope for; it is our conviction about things that we cannot see.

(Moffatt)

Now faith means that we are confident of what we hope for, convinced of what we do not see.

(Berkeley)

But faith forms a solid ground for what is hoped for, a conviction of unseen realities.

(Beck)

Faith is being sure of the things we hope for, being convinced of the things we can't see.

(Montgomery)

Now faith is a title-deed of things hoped for; the putting to the proof of things not seen.

(New English Bible)

And what is faith? Faith gives substance to our hopes, and makes us certain of realities we do not see.

(Twentieth Century New Testament)

Faith is the realization of things hoped for—the proof of things not seen.

(Williams)

Now faith is the assurance of the things we hope for, the proof of the reality of the things we cannot see.

(Amplified)

Now faith is the assurance (the confirmation, the title-deed) of the things [we] hope for, being the proof of things [we] do not see and the conviction of their reality [faith perceiving as real fact what is not revealed to the senses].

Find Out What Faith Is Not

Sometimes to accurately define and identify something, we must first find out what it is *not*. In fact, sometimes it is easier to find out what something is when you find out what it is not. It is then easier to discover what it actually is.

In the mechanical shop at RHEMA, sometimes rather than looking for the problem, the mechanics begin to sort out what the problem is by determining what it is not. By finding out through the process of elimination what the problem is *not*, they are able to determine what the problem is.

For example, if the problem is in the electrical system, they can determine, "Well, the problem is definitely not in the fuel system. And we know it's not in the oil system," and they list what the problem is *not*.

They can check out various systems and determine, "It's not this. It's not this or this." And as they run through the systems, after a while, they are able to determine what the problem is through the process of elimination.

We can do the same thing spiritually when it comes to faith. It is important to look at what biblical faith is *not*, so we can determine what biblical faith in God *is*. If we can grasp what faith is *not*, we can have a better understanding of what faith *is*. Then we can use our faith to be stronger individually and corporately as a body of believers.

Listed below are some things that faith is *not*:

Faith is not an isolated spiritual force; in other words, faith works in connection with other spiritual forces.

Faith is not denial; it does not deny the existence of a problem.

Faith is not neglect; it does not neglect responsibilities.

Faith is not imitation. Faith cannot be imitated; it must arise in each person's heart based on the Word of God.

Faith is not a legalistic formula. God responds to faith, not to formulas.

Faith is not an issue of ordering God around. Faith does not negate the sovereignty of God.

Faith is not a ticket to Utopia. Faith does not ensure perfection for this life.

Faith is not a panic button to push only in times of trouble; it is a lifestyle of trusting in God.

Faith is not a magic wand; faith doesn't instantly settle every problem or question.

Faith is not the ability to override the free will of another; faith does not give us authority over other people.

Faith is not limited to specific results; we must also have a general underlying faith that cannot be moved by any circumstance.

Faith is not the absence of feeling; faith is based on the Word, not on feeling, but faith does not deny the existence of feelings.

Faith Is a Spiritual Force

First of all, we have to understand that faith is a spiritual force. In other words, faith is a spiritual issue; it is not a natural issue. Faith is of man's *spirit*, not of his *mind* or *body*.

When we are dealing with faith *in* God, faith *from* God, and the faith *of* God, we must realize that God is Spirit (John 4:24). Therefore, faith in Him is a spiritual issue to be discerned and operated spiritually.

The Bible says that we are spirit beings. Man is a spirit, he has a soul, and he lives in a body. So Bible faith is of man's recreated spirit, not his mind or flesh.

> **1 THESSALONIANS 5:23**
> **23 And the very God of peace sanctify you wholly; and I pray God your whole SPIRIT and SOUL and BODY be preserved blameless unto the coming of our Lord Jesus Christ.**

That's why Bible faith is of man's heart or recreated spirit; it is not mental. It is a spiritual force! The Bible calls it "the spirit of faith."

> **2 CORINTHIANS 4:13**
> **13 We having the same SPIRIT OF FAITH, according as it is written, I BELIEVED, and therefore have I SPOKEN; we also BELIEVE, and therefore SPEAK.**

What is the spirit of faith? It's Bible faith—*believing* with the heart and *speaking* with the mouth.

In another scripture, the Bible says that faith is *believing* with the heart and *confessing* with the mouth.

> **ROMANS 10:9,10**
> **9   That if thou shalt CONFESS WITH THY MOUTH the Lord Jesus, and shalt BELIEVE IN THINE HEART that God hath raised him from the dead, thou shalt be saved.**
> **10 For WITH THE HEART MAN BELIEVETH unto righteousness; and with THE MOUTH CONFESSION IS MADE unto salvation.**

The Bible talks about the "hidden man of the heart" or man's spirit. Faith in God resides in the hidden man of the heart, man's spirit.

> **1 PETER 3:4**
> **4   But let it be the HIDDEN MAN OF THE HEART, in that which is not corruptible, even the ornament of a meek and quiet spirit, which is in the sight of God of great price.**

In other words, man believes with his heart or spirit. So biblical faith is not mental; it is not mental assent. It is not intellectual agreement. Faith is a spiritual force that grows and develops in the heart or spirit of man.

Jesus said that His Word is spirit and life (John 6:63). Therefore, Bible faith comes from God's Word: ". . . *faith cometh by hearing, and hearing by the word of God*" (Rom. 10:17). God's Word has the ability to quicken us spiritually.

JOHN 6:63
63 It is the spirit that quickeneth; the flesh prof-
iteth nothing: the words that I speak unto you,
THEY ARE SPIRIT, and THEY ARE LIFE.

Since the Word of God is spirit, it has the ability to
produce a spiritual force within our hearts called
"faith." Faith in God's Word can change circumstances
and move impossible "mountains" in our lives
(Mark 11:23,24).

As we hear the "logos" or the written Word of God, it
develops faith inside of us. We believe the logos—the
written Word of God. Then as we speak the *logos* Word
of God, in a sense it becomes a *rhema* Word of God to us.

The word "rhema" is a Greek word. In its literal
sense, it simply means "speaking" or "the spoken word."
So in the sense we are using it, "rhema" means the Word
of God spoken. The Word of God that is spoken out in
faith becomes the "rhema" Word—*the spoken Word.*

Vine's Expository Dictionary of Biblical Words
defines "rhema" in the following way:

> The significance of *rhema* (as distinct from *logos*) is
> exemplified in the injunction to take "the sword of the
> Spirit, which is the word of God," Eph. 6:17; here the
> reference is not to the whole Bible as such, but to the
> individual scripture which the Spirit brings to our
> remembrance for use in time of need, a prerequisite
> being the regular storing of the mind with Scripture.[1]

Therefore, the *rhema* Word of God—the Word of God
spoken—is a spiritual force. It must be dealt with spiritually. For example, unless you understand it spiritually,

there is no way to explain the *rhema* word of God because the Bible says that spiritual things are spiritually discerned. You won't be able to discern spiritual things with just your natural mind.

> **1 CORINTHIANS 2:14**
> **14 But the NATURAL MAN receiveth not the things of the Spirit of God: for they are foolishness unto him: neither can he know them, because they are SPIRITUALLY DISCERNED.**

Spiritual things are not discerned by the natural man—by man's mind and intellect. That's why many people have problems understanding spiritual things. They try to understand the things of God with only their natural mind.

Faith Is Not an Isolated Spiritual Force

Faith is a spiritual force, but it is not an *isolated* spiritual force. That means faith was never meant to work alone, just by itself. It works in conjunction with other spiritual forces of God such as love and patience.

You see, spiritual forces must operate in context with other spiritual forces to work. When you study the Word, you see that faith was intended to operate with other spiritual forces of God.

For example, prayer is a spiritual force; scriptural prayer releases the power of God. Faith operates with prayer. When you pray in faith, you receive your answer from God. But it takes faith to activate prayer.

The love of God is also a spiritual force, but it takes love to make faith operate. The Bible said, "faith works by love" (Gal. 5:6).

All the spiritual forces that God has set into existence—love, prayer, hope, patience—must operate together in order to accomplish the purposes of God.

The natural and the spiritual must also function together. For example, each of us has a human body. We understand that the Bible said we are a spirit, we have a soul, and we live in a body (1 Thess. 5:23). To function properly in the natural and in the spiritual realms, man's threefold nature—spirit, soul, and body—must work together.

Then in the natural realm, all the bodily systems must function properly and work together too. For example, the human body has a circulatory system, a respiratory system, a digestive system, a central nervous system, and so on. Even though all those systems are different and operate separately, they must also operate together in harmony to allow the body to function properly.

That's the way faith is. Faith is not an isolated force, operating alone. Faith is a spiritual force that must function in unity and harmony with the other spiritual forces that God has set into motion such as love, hope, patience, and prayer.

The Word Is Food to Our Spirit

Since the Word of God is Spirit and life, the Word is spiritual sustenance—bread—to our spirits.

MATTHEW 4:4
4 But he answered and said, It is written, Man shall not live by bread alone, but by EVERY WORD that proceedeth out of the mouth of God.

The Bible says man is to live by ". . . *every word that proceedeth out of the mouth of God.*" Why does God want us to live by His Word? One reason is that faith comes by hearing the Word of God. Therefore, faith cannot operate independently of the Word.

Some believers want to pick a few isolated words out of the Bible and live just by those words. For example, they want to pick out healing and prosperity scriptures and use those scriptures as their scriptural foundation.

Well, it's true that scriptures on healing and prosperity are words that proceed out of God's mouth, and we can live by them. But we also need all the other scriptures in God's Word to live by! Basing our lives on one or two scriptures would be like trying to live in the natural realm by just eating one or two kinds of foods. It won't work.

And often people who pick and choose the scriptures they want to live by are not too eager to find scriptures about holiness, consecration, evangelism, judgment, and the love of God. However, faith and prosperity, holiness, consecration, evangelism, judgment, and the love of God all work together to develop a mature spiritual man. The Word helps man walk with God, receive from God, and fulfill God's will on the earth.

But all that many people want is just to receive from God. They continually pray, "God, gimme, gimme,

gimme . . ." Yes, the Word of God does talk about receiving from God. And it's true that we can't give out to others until we have received something from God ourselves.

But we cannot just take portions and bits and pieces from the Bible and develop into strong, mature Christians. We need the whole counsel of God, not just part of it. The whole counsel of God must work together in our lives to develop a strong spiritual man.

Faith is important to our spiritual development because the Bible says that we are to live by faith (Rom. 1:17). But we must also live a life of love because faith works by love.

Sometimes it seems that people who tend to talk the most about how much faith they have and what strong "faith people" they are often don't seem to have much love. But since faith works together with love to be effective, strong faith is impossible without love.

> **1 CORINTHIANS 13:13**
> **13 And now abideth faith, hope, charity** [or love], **these three; but the greatest of these is charity** [love].

According to some people, the greatest spiritual quality is faith. But the Bible doesn't say that. It says, ". . . the greatest of these is *love*." However, the Bible does say, "faith works by love" (Gal. 5:6). Therefore, both faith and love must work together to be efficient. But love is more important than faith, because love is the catalyst that gets faith working.

If you don't have love, your faith is not going to work! That's one reason some people have a hard time using their faith. They can quote the Word, and they brag about how much they believe God, but they still don't seem to be receiving from Him. It may be that they lack love.

My dad says the first place he tells people to look when they don't seem to be receiving from God is their love walk. You see, faith cannot be an isolated spiritual force. Faith does not work alone. Faith works in connection with all of the other spiritual forces of God, and one of those is love. Love working together with faith causes faith to operate properly.

For example, using the illustration of an automobile again, a car has many different systems: an electrical system, a fuel system, a cooling system, just to name a few. All of those systems work independently of each other, but to make the automobile run smoothly, all the systems must also work together properly.

Even though a car has many independent systems, you're going to have a problem if the cooling system breaks down or the oil system doesn't work. All systems must work efficiently separately before they can work together collectively. For instance, if the cooling system or the oil system shuts down, your engine is going to blow!

Some believers have blown up their faith "system" by failing to walk in love! Because one area affects another area, failing to walk in love can almost shut down someone's spiritual walk with the Lord.

Faith and Patience Work Together

Faith works with other qualities too. When our faith is tested and tried as we continue to stand on the Word, it works patience in our lives.

> **JAMES 1:2–4**
> 2 My brethren, count it all joy when ye fall into divers temptations;
> 3 Knowing this, that the trying of your FAITH WORKETH PATIENCE.
> 4 But let patience have her perfect work, that ye may be perfect and entire, wanting nothing.

The Bible says we cannot inherit the promises of God without patience. Therefore, faith and patience work together to help us receive what we need from God.

> **HEBREWS 6:12**
> 12 That ye be not slothful, but followers of them who through FAITH AND PATIENCE inherit the promises.

You can see that patience is another quality or spiritual force that interacts with faith. When patience is fully developed, it perfects our faith. But patience is something most people don't like because it requires some endurance!

Many people say they want to develop strong faith. But if they're going to develop strong, enduring faith, they must "let patience have her perfect work" because patience perfects or matures our faith.

You can see the need for patience in another scripture too. The Bible says there will be times we must stand on the Word regardless of circumstances. Sometimes that takes patient endurance.

EPHESIANS 6:13,14
13 Wherefore take unto you the whole armour of God, that ye may be able to withstand in the evil day, and having done all, TO STAND.
14 STAND THEREFORE....

The answers to our petitions don't always manifest overnight. When we don't see immediate results, those are the times we just have to stand on God's promises, even in the midst of negative circumstances. That takes patience!

When you do everything you know to stand in faith, and then you keep on standing—patience is perfecting your faith and making it strong. You may have to endure some tests in order to keep on standing, but if you patiently stand steadfast on God's Word, you will see your answer.

Many believers don't want to keep on standing; they want the answer *now*. They don't want to wait or to "let patience have her perfect work." They just want the answer quick and easy—*right now* without any effort!

A couple of years ago, I read that Tulsa, Oklahoma, is the fast-food capital of the world. More people per capita eat at fast-food restaurants in Tulsa than anywhere else in the world.

You see, we live in a "now" society. We want everything now! It seems to be the spirit of the age. For example, if we have a computer, as soon as an updated model is available, we want the updated version right away so it will run faster. We want the faster, upgraded models so we can produce more work more quickly—*now*!

When we buy a new car, one of the questions many men ask is "How many seconds does it take to go from zero to 60?" Or "How fast can it run the quarter mile?" They'll probably never use that zero to 60 speed because traffic doesn't allow them to go that fast anyway!

But sometimes people ask, "What's the highest speed your car will go?"

"Oh, this one will go about 145 miles an hour."

Where in the world could we ever drive at 145 miles an hour unless we are on a racetrack? But, you see, if we are not careful, we can get caught up in the spirit of this age and want everything fast, quick, and easy—right now! But God's Word says it takes patience or steadfast endurance to inherit the promises of God (Heb. 6:12).

When we get caught up in the world's impatience, it hinders us from walking in the faith of God. We need patience to mature our faith and make it strong and stable. Then nothing can cause us to falter in our faith walk with God.

Add Other Qualities to Your Faith

The Bible says we are to add other spiritual qualities to our faith. There is a reason for this. Other spiritual qualities strengthen our faith.

> **2 PETER 1:5-9**
> **5 And beside this, giving all DILIGENCE, ADD TO YOUR FAITH VIRTUE; and to virtue KNOWLEDGE;**

6 And to knowledge TEMPERANCE; and to temperance PATIENCE; and to patience GODLINESS;
7 And to godliness BROTHERLY KINDNESS; and to brotherly kindness CHARITY [or love].
8 For IF THESE THINGS BE IN YOU, and abound, they make you that ye shall neither be barren nor unfruitful in the knowledge of our Lord Jesus Christ.
9 But he that lacketh these things is blind, and cannot see afar off, and hath forgotten that he was purged from his old sins.

You see, faith is not an isolated spiritual force or quality. It works with other spiritual qualities. In fact, not only do you need patience to develop your faith, you also need diligence, virtue, knowledge, temperance, brotherly kindness, and love. If you add these qualities to your faith, your faith won't be barren or unfruitful. It will produce for you!

The Bible says, *"And beside this, giving all diligence, add to your faith virtue . . ."* (v. 5). The word "diligence" means to give special attention to something by persistence. It means you stay with something, stick to it, and persevere even when circumstances are against you.

So we could read Second Peter 1:5: "And besides this, add persistence and perseverance to your faith."

Many believers have studied the Word and increased their faith, but they don't seem to be receiving all they should from believing God. Many times their problem is that they have not added these other qualities to their faith. These other spiritual qualities would greatly strengthen their faith, but some believers try to operate their faith in an isolated spiritual cocoon.

Faith is vitally important because you can't please God without it (Heb. 11:6). But faith is not an isolated spiritual force to be used or developed alone. That's why the Bible tells us to add these other qualities to our faith. These other spiritual qualities strengthen and transform our faith to make it enduring and strong even in tests and trials.

Our faith in God is valuable. In fact, the Bible says the trying of our faith is more precious than gold (1 Peter 1:7). Therefore, the faith of God should be held in high esteem. But faith must grow and develop so it can be increased. We must develop exceedingly growing faith so we can accomplish everything God has for us in this life.

But along with increasing and developing our faith, we must also seek to grow in love, wisdom, hope, patience, virtue, knowledge, and temperance, since all these qualities cooperate with and complement faith.

You see, faith is not an isolated spiritual force to be used in an isolated fashion—in a vacuum. Don't misunderstand me. In order to understand faith, you may have to study it by isolating it. But you put faith into action and make it work by combining it with love, patience, virtue, knowledge, and temperance. All these other qualities give faith its strength and make faith work.

Too many times believers study faith alright, but they don't bother to study it in conjunction with all the other spiritual qualities designed to work with faith. But when they learn to add these other qualities to their faith, they can start consistently receiving answers from God.

We do not need to shrink back from faith! We need to stand stronger in faith on God's Word than ever before. But use wisdom and unite faith with these other spiritual qualities. That's how we will become so strong in faith that no wind of doctrine or any devil in hell can move us! We become rooted and grounded firmly in God's Word!

Faith is a supernatural force, but we live in a natural world. In fact, we live in a spiritual world and a natural world at the same time. Therefore, we must use our supernatural faith to operate in a natural world.

How can we operate successfully in both worlds? As we stand on God's Word, faith will bring results in both realms—in both the spiritual and the natural realms. Standing on God's Word in the spiritual realm enables us to live successfully in the natural world.

After all, we will have to operate in both worlds as long as we draw breath on this earth. So we can stand on God's Word and speak out the *rhema* Word of God to change our circumstances.

I've said for many years that the natural and the supernatural coming together produce an explosive force for God! Put God's Word to work for you in your life. Speak God's Word over your family, your church, and your community. If you put God's Word to work for you, you can change your world!

Stir your faith up to believe God more than you've ever believed Him before. Rekindle the excitement of taking God at His Word. But be diligent to add the qualities of patient endurance, virtue, knowledge, and temperance to your faith so you can begin receiving everything God promised you in His Word!

---

[1] W.E. Vine, Merrill F. Unger, William White, Jr. eds. Vine's Expository Dictionary of Biblical Words (Thomas Nelson Publishers: Nashville, 1985), p. 1242

Chapter 2
Faith Is Not Denial

So then FAITH COMETH BY HEARING, and hearing by THE WORD OF GOD.

—Romans 10:17

And Jesus answering saith unto them, HAVE FAITH IN GOD.

For verily I say unto you, That whosoever shall say unto this mountain, Be thou removed, and be thou cast into the sea; and shall not doubt in his heart, but shall believe that those things which he saith shall come to pass; he shall have whatsoever he saith.

Therefore I say unto you, What things soever ye desire, when ye pray, believe that ye receive them, and ye shall have them.

—Mark 11:22–24

God wants us to have faith in Him! Mark 11:22 can also be translated, "Have the faith of God." You see, faith in God is a spiritual force. It comes by hearing the Word of God. The force of faith—Bible faith—can change your circumstances. But what is Bible faith?

To help answer that question, let's continue to look at what Bible faith is *not*.

Faith Does Not Deny Circumstances

We need to take another look at faith because some believers are confused about what Bible faith really is. Some think that faith is denying the problem, sickness, disease, or the hindrance. But faith is not denial! Denying the existence of a problem is *not* faith—it's foolishness!

Some people think that as long as they don't speak about a problem, that means they are in faith. Faith pleases God, so they think by denying a problem, they are pleasing God because they are acting in faith.

But faith—Bible faith—does not deny the existence or the reality of a problem. In some situations it is very dangerous to deny that a problem exists, especially in the case of sickness and disease.

Some people even say, "I will not admit that I have a problem because I don't want to confess it into existence." But by admitting a problem, they aren't confessing the problem into existence—the problem is already there!

For example, suppose you have all the symptoms of a cold—your nose is running, your eyes are watering, you have a fever, and you are sneezing and coughing. But instead of admitting you have a cold, you confess, "I don't have any symptoms. I'm fine. Nothing is the matter with me." That's not faith—that's lying!

Some people think they are standing in faith for healing by just making confessions that deny the fact that they are sick. But everyone else can see that they *are* sick because they use a box of tissues every fifteen minutes and eat cough drops like candy! But in an effort to be in faith, many people will still confess, "Nothing is wrong with me! I'm not going to confess that I am sick."

But you don't have to confess it when it is plain to see that you are sick! The facts speak for themselves.

You see, merely confessing or not confessing something doesn't change the *facts*. Now if you put the Word of God to work, eventually your circumstances are subject to change. But some people have the mistaken idea, "If I don't acknowledge my problem as a fact, then I haven't *confessed* it. And if I don't *confess* it, it must disappear."

But the Bible doesn't say, "Deny the truth. Don't confess the facts." It says to confess *those things* that be *not* as though they were (Rom. 4:17). And for some things, it doesn't matter whether you confess them or not; they still exist as *fact*.

If you are broke, it's a fact whether you confess it or not. Whether or not you confess it to anyone, you are still broke. You won't get out of that situation until you recognize that fact, and then put your faith to work for you.

It's the same way with healing. A person has to recognize he is sick before he can get healed. And a person has to recognize the fact that he is a sinner before he can get saved.

Therefore, the quicker you recognize the facts that exist and apply the greater facts of God's Word to the situation, the quicker you will be delivered!

For example, one fellow who was divorced said, "I will never confess that I am divorced. You will never hear that spoken from my lips."

I said, "You don't have to confess you are divorced. It's a fact that is recorded down at the county courthouse."

He thought that by denying the fact that he was divorced, God could restore his marriage. But I explained to him that before a person can believe God to move in his behalf, he must realize that a problem exists!

For example, before you could get saved, you had to realize you were a sinner. You had to realize you needed a Savior! Before you can get healed, you must realize you have a physical problem.

But so many people think that faith is denying the facts. They think that by denying the facts, their faith is working. But the Bible does not teach this.

Look at the Old Testament men of faith. In an effort to be in faith, did they deny their problems? Did Joshua deny the existence of Jericho that lay in front of him to be defeated? No! He knew that enemy fortress lay ahead of him. In other words, he admitted to that obstacle or problem.

But Joshua didn't stop there! Then Joshua acted in faith on what God had told him to do. The children of Israel shouted, and the walls came tumbling down.

When David was confronted with Goliath, did David deny the existence of the giant standing before him cursing God?

No! By faith in God, David ran out to defeat his enemy (*see* First Samuel chapter 17).

So many people want to stick their head in the sand spiritually speaking, and deny that they have a problem. But if your pockets are empty, you've got empty pockets! You might as well admit it. But then don't stop there. Those empty pockets don't have to *stay* empty! Use those empty pockets as an opportunity to prove that God's Word works!

Arm yourself with the greater facts of God's Word and by faith begin to say what God's Word says about your particular situation: "My God shall supply all my need according to His riches in glory by Christ Jesus" (Phil. 4:19). Don't deny the facts, but allow God's Word to transform and change those facts!

Look at the woman with the issue of blood (Mark 5:25–34). She did not deny the fact that she needed healing. She didn't just sit in her house denying the fact that she'd had this condition for twelve years.

She didn't deny the fact that the physicians could not cure her. She did not deny the fact that she'd only grown worse, but she didn't just wallow in her problem either. No, she recognized that she had a problem, but then she did something about it!

She used her faith to look beyond her problem to Jesus. She allowed the greater fact of Jesus, the Living Word of God, to overcome her problem. She said, "If I can touch the hem of Jesus' garment, I will be made whole" (Matt. 9:21). That was her faith talking!

But notice that she didn't just make that confession and then sit still doing nothing. Faith is an *act*—it's *acting* on God's Word. It's taking God at His Word and acting like it is true. So she acted on her faith by getting up and going to Jesus! Even though she was still afflicted with an issue of blood, she knew when she touched the hem of Jesus' garment, she'd be healed.

Faith Faces the 'What Ifs' of Life With Victory!

Study the lives of great men and women of faith in the Bible. All of them—Abraham, Isaac, Jacob, Gideon, Esther, Daniel, just to name a few—were confronted with problems that had to be overcome. But they faced their problems with a strong belief in God and triumphed over every insurmountable barrier!

Faith is not afraid to face problems, obstacles, and difficulties. It doesn't draw back in fear. Faith presses on to God and wins the victory every single time!

Faith is not afraid to face the perplexities of life either—the "what ifs" of life. For example, we've probably all heard people say in fear, "Yes, but *what if* . . . ?" But when you are in faith, you can fearlessly face every problem or trial with confidence. Faith looks at negative situations and declares, "I am not afraid of the 'what ifs' because God is bigger than any problem or circumstance! I serve a great, big God who can overcome anything!"

Now it's easy to say that God will take care of you when you are sitting snug and secure in your church surrounded by other strong believers. But it's another thing to say, "God will take care of me" when turmoil surrounds you, you can't pay the rent, and the electricity is about to be shut off!

You can talk about how much faith you've got while you are safe and secure in the comforts of your own home. But it's another thing to act in faith when nothing is going right, and your only hope is God. One Bible translation says, "You show me your faith without any action, and I'll show you my faith by my action" (James 2:18).

Believers who are tested but stand firm on God's Word in the face of negative situations show their faith by their action. True faith in God does not waver in times of trouble.

Remember a woman in the Bible by the name of Esther? She faced a dangerous situation; not only was her own life in peril, but the entire nation of Israel was faced with extinction. The wicked Haman had devised a plot to kill all the Jews in the kingdom and also to destroy the Jewish Queen Esther.

So Esther faced not only the extinction of her race, but also the loss of her own life. Yet in the midst of almost sure destruction, she stood fast, trusting in God. She demonstrated her great faith in God by her action. She did all she could in the natural, but then she cast the care on God by saying, ". . . *if I perish, I perish*" (Esther 4:16). That was her commitment.

Many times in the Word of God people obeyed God and went against all odds, yet they received their victories. For example, in reality, it didn't make any sense for Gideon to go out to battle with 300 men against an army of more than 20,000 trained fighting men. But he did what God told him to do, and Israel won the victory that day (*see* Judges chapter 7)!

And in reality, Daniel should have been eaten alive when he was thrown into the lion's den (Dan. 6:16). But Daniel faced that perilous situation armed only with his faith in God. The angel of the Lord protected Daniel so that the lions slept peacefully that night, and Daniel came out the victor!

In fact, King Darius had Daniel's accusers thrown into the lion's den instead. His accusers were torn to pieces by the very same lions—before those men ever hit the bottom of the pit (Dan. 6:24). In one day, Daniel's enemies were destroyed, but Daniel prospered (Dan. 6:28).

Every one of the great men and women of faith in the Bible faced problems in life. Faith won't keep you from experiencing some problems. But each one of these faith giants we read about in the Word did something about their problems. They put their trust in God, stepped out in obedience to do what God told them, and God brought them through victoriously.

Do You Really Believe God?

You will have to learn whether you really believe God or whether you are just talking a good talk. You find out how much you believe God when you come up against dangerous situations and your life is on the line.

I remember years ago when I went to Africa with another minister. We'd chartered a small airplane to go from one city in Kenya to another. As we started our descent to land at our destination, we could see a bad storm rolling in.

The pilot of that small aircraft quickly landed the plane on a grassy strip, threw our luggage out, and said, "There's a road. You can catch a vehicle going into town. It's only a few kilometers. Go to the hotel, and there will be someone who speaks English to help you. I've got to get out of the way of that approaching storm."

It was about 5:30 in the evening, and the shadows were gathering as the night approached. Here were two preachers who hadn't slept for about eighteen hours, standing alone beside a road that led to a remote town we knew nothing about. We did not even know where we were, except that we were somewhere in Kenya!

You find out how much you believe God in circumstances like that! When we were finally picked up, we found ourselves in the back of a truck with some rough-looking men who continually eyed our cameras and luggage. We couldn't understand what they were saying, but we knew they wanted our gear.

We found out later how dangerous it is in that part of the world to ride into town with strangers! But we didn't know that at the time, and God protected us.

Making Faith Declarations

When that minister and I had first landed in Africa, as we walked across the tarmac to customs, we prayed in agreement. We made a faith declaration. We prayed,

"In the Name of Jesus, while we are in this country, no harm will befall us. And besides that, we will not be bitten by any insects or anything else that would harm us!"

I remembered that faith declaration as I thought about the Lord's protection that day. We finally arrived at that village and hired a taxi to drive us to our destination. We found out later that was something else you don't do unless you know the taxicab driver. But we didn't know any better, and once again God protected us.

We had to believe God every step of the way on that trip. It rained horribly that night as we taxied from one city to another. At one point, I woke up just as that cab was sliding and skidding down the road.

Later when I drove back over those same roads, I saw that we were high up in the mountains, and on one side, there was a thousand-foot cliff! I thought, *Lord, You were so good to protect us. We didn't even know we needed protecting!*

You find out just how strong your faith is when you lie down at night and turn out the light and you hear, "Bzzz, bzzz." All those bugs that we'd claimed wouldn't bite us buzzed around constantly in our room.

In the United States, those insects probably aren't dangerous. But in many places in Africa, mosquitoes can carry malaria. However, God protected us, and we weren't bitten or harmed in any way.

But, you see, it's one thing to talk about having faith and believing God. It's another thing to live your faith in God when you are faced with dangerous situations.

Sometimes we face minor problems in life that we overcome with our faith. But when your life is on the line, you find out how much faith in God you really have!

Faith in God Overcomes Problems!

Faith in God does not mean you will never face another problem. Faith in God simply means you know how to deal with problems and triumph over them. Everyone is confronted with problems from time to time in life. But your faith in God allows you to overcome problems—not to be overcome by them.

Actually, the first step to victory is recognizing that you have a problem! Only then can you begin to use your faith to reverse the situation! You see, faith is not denial. That's why you must first identify the problem. *Then* put your faith to work for you. Nothing is too hard for God! But if you never admit you have a problem, you'll never put your faith to work against the problem. Faith does not deny the existence of problems; it just overcomes them by the power of God's Word!

When you are in faith, you realize that problems exist, but you know the greater truth of God's Word that says, *"But thanks be to God, which giveth us the victory through our Lord Jesus Christ"* (1 Cor. 15:57). You know you don't have to be defeated by problems!

Faith—Bible faith—is a matter of making a choice to believe God's Word rather than the problems that confront you. Yes, you will have to stand on God's Word until the problems come in line with the Word.

But you don't have to be defeated by problems and negative circumstances!

And sometimes standing on the Word in the midst of trials requires some perseverance and patience. But having done all to stand on God's Word, then begin declaring your faith: "God said it. I believe it! Therefore, I receive my petition according to the Word of God, and I count it as done!"

When you can't see your answer, feel it, touch it, or taste it—you must still stand on God's Word, praising Him that He has already answered your prayers! That's real faith in God! Thank God, He will meet your every need.

I don't mean to minimize the problems that confront all of us from time to time. And little problems are just as real to someone as a tremendously big problem is to someone else. We all face problems in life no matter who we are. But what I am saying is that God is bigger than any problems!

But, you see, it is easy to believe God when everything is going smoothly. But strong faith believes God even when things go wrong and the pressures of life seem to press in on every side. And your faith in God will always be rewarded by victory if you'll just persevere in God!

Neglecting Your Health Is Not Faith

People also mistake faith for neglect in the area of taking care of their health. They think they can neglect their body and just pray and God will take care of them. But God also expects us to use some common sense.

For example, in the wintertime when I'm preaching on a platform where those hot stage lights generate so much heat, it would be foolish of me to immediately go outside without a coat! It would not be faith to just say, "Well, I'm preaching the Word, so God will take care of me."

We still need to use some common sense! Faith does not negate common sense, and it doesn't mean we can neglect taking care of our physical bodies. If I leave the platform hot and sweaty and wear my coat so I can greet my congregation at the door where the cold wind blows on me, does that mean I don't have any faith? No, it means I've got some sense!

People who neglect their physical bodies in the name of "faith" need to ask God's forgiveness before they ask for healing! Some believers are always needing God to heal them because they've neglected using common sense, and they've acted foolishly.

Sometimes God blesses us in spite of our ignorance, but He expects us to learn and grow spiritually! We need to realize that we have a responsibility to take care of ourselves too. We just can't keep pushing our bodies, or we can begin to develop physical symptoms.

PHILIPPIANS 2:25–27,30
**25 Yet I supposed it necessary to send to you Epa-
phroditus, my brother, and companion in labour,
and fellowsoldier, but your messenger, and he that
ministered to my wants.**

> 26 For he longed after you all, and was full of heaviness, because that ye had heard that he had been sick.
> 27 For indeed he was sick nigh unto death: but God had mercy on him; and not on him only, but on me also, lest I should have sorrow upon sorrow. . . .
> 30 Because for the work of Christ he was nigh unto death, not regarding his life, to supply your lack of service toward me.

The *Wuest* translation says that Epaphroditus "recklessly exposed his life" (v. 30). Many Bible scholars say that Epaphroditus got into trouble because he overworked in the ministry and neglected his own health.

His intentions were good; he was working for the Lord. But nevertheless, Epaphroditus neglected taking care of his body properly, so it began to give him trouble.

Epaphroditus had helped Paul greatly in the ministry. If Paul had lost Epaphroditus, his fellow laborer, he would have been sorrowful. That's why Paulsaid, ". . . *lest I should have sorrow upon sorrow"* (v. 27).

But Paul not only would have been sorry to lose Epaphroditus, he probably would have also felt responsible for allowing this fellow minister to overwork.

We've got to take care of ourselves! Taking good care of our bodies doesn't hinder our faith. Not taking care of our bodies can hinder our faith because then we're always sick and have to spend all our time trying to get healed—and we wonder why!

We cannot recklessly expose ourselves to danger and risk our health. For example, if you visit someone who has a contagious disease, the doctors require you to wear a mask to protect yourself.

But some believers who consider themselves such great "faith" people say, "Bless God! I'm a person of faith. I don't need any protection except my faith!"

That's just ignorance! In my life, I've believed God and received some tremendous answers to prayer. Yes, my faith in the Word protects me, but I also have to use some common sense! I can't neglect my responsibilities to take care of myself in the natural in the name of "faith" and act foolishly.

I do all I can in the natural, and then based on the promises in His Word, I expect God to take care of me in the supernatural.

For example, if I were visiting a person who had a contagious disease and doctors told me, "We recommend that you put on a gown and mask for your own protection," I would have enough sense to do what they recommend! It wouldn't hinder my faith at all to protect myself as I prayed the prayer of faith for the sick person to be healed!

Many believers do foolish things and call it faith, when really they are just acting in ignorance! Faith is not neglect!

You can't neglect your health and at the same time try to have faith for your health. In other words, as you believe God for good health, don't neglect your responsibility to get the proper exercise, rest, and nutrition. Neglecting the natural realm while you're trying to believe God in the supernatural realm is not faith—it's foolishness!

Faith vs. Medical Care

What about faith versus medical care? Some believers think it shows a lack of faith to go to the doctor when they are sick. But think about the wonderful discoveries made by medical science! For instance, medication can help people stay alive as they build their faith in the Word to believe for their healing.

If you happen to be in that category of those needing medication, I suggest you continue to take your medicine according to your medical prescription as you build your faith in God's Word. Taking medication shouldn't negate your faith that God is still working in the situation.

Actually, sometimes doctors can keep you alive until you can activate your faith! God is the One who gave doctors the knowledge to discover all those wonderful medical breakthroughs in the first place! So do all you can in the natural and do all you can in the supernatural by standing strong on God's Word.

Brother O.B. Braun in Fort Worth, Texas, was a good example of a person who built up his faith while he continued to take his medicine. Brother Braun was a full-time minister friend of my dad's. He has since gone to be with the Lord, but over the years, my dad held many revival meetings for him.

Brother Braun had sugar diabetes for about thirty years. Every morning he had to check his blood sugar level and give himself a shot of the proper dosage of insulin. But finally Brother Braun learned how to believe God for his own healing by standing on the Word.

When he learned how to activate his faith in God's Word, he would give himself an insulin shot, then make this faith declaration: "I thank You, God, that You are working in my body to effect a healing and a cure in Jesus' Name."

After he'd been standing on God's Word in faith for a while, his doctor checked him out again. His doctor asked him, "Could you stay at the hospital a little longer so we can run a few more tests? Something has changed."

Brother Braun realized that for the last several days he hadn't needed to take any insulin at all. His doctor ran all the tests on him and couldn't find anything wrong with him.

Finally he told Brother Braun, "I've been your doctor all these years. And in all these years, you've always needed to take insulin. But now your pancreas is working normally and supplying your own insulin, so you don't need to take insulin shots anymore."

From that time until years later when he went on to be with the Lord, Brother Braun never took any more insulin. He didn't need to because he was totally healed. But, you see, it didn't hinder his faith at all to take those insulin shots while he was believing God for his healing.

Every time he took his medication, he just declared in faith that God was working in the situation. Actually, the medication kept him alive while he fought the good fight of faith—and won!

Many people say that those of us who believe in God's Word are against medical doctors. But we are not. In fact, Brother Hagin has said, "If you don't have faith to be healed, you need to go to the doctor. Take your medicine so you can stay alive until you build your faith so you can receive your healing."

Someone said, "But I have an incurable disease." Well, medicine can make life a lot easier for you while you are standing on God's Word for your healing!

Do we see anything about medicine in the Bible? Yes, remember the parable Jesus told about the Good Samaritan and the wounded man left for dead by the side of the road (Luke 10:30–37). What did the Good Samaritan do when he found the injured man? He ministered to him the only way he knew how.

> **LUKE 10:30–35**
> **30 And Jesus answering said, A certain man went down from Jerusalem to Jericho, and fell among thieves, which stripped him of his raiment, and wounded him, and departed, leaving him half dead.**
> **31 And by chance there came down a certain priest that way: and when he saw him, he passed by on the other side.**
> **32 And likewise a Levite, when he was at the place, came and looked on him, and passed by on the other side.**
> **33 But a certain Samaritan, as he journeyed, came where he was: and when he saw him, he had compassion on him,**
> **34 And went to him, and bound up his wounds, POURING IN OIL AND WINE, and set him on his own beast, and brought him to an inn, and took care of him.**

35 And on the morrow when he departed, he took out two pence, and gave them to the host, and said unto him, Take care of him; and whatsoever thou spendest more, when I come again, I will repay thee.

Probably today we would say the Good Samaritan ministered first aid to this man. He cleaned his wounds by using oil and wine, which not only disinfected the wound but acted as a balm to seal the wound against further infection. That was the best medication that was available to him. Then he bandaged him up and took him to an inn.

Jesus mentioned the Good Samaritan's deed as commendable, not lacking in faith. Sometimes I think people overreact against doctors and medicine. But, the truth is, doctors and medicine are one way God has of trying to help people who don't know anything about faith!

God created man, and He is interested in man's welfare. Some people have suffered unnecessarily because they thought that to be in faith, they had to refuse medical help.

I remember something that happened when my cousin Ruth lived with us when she was a teenager. She once had an appendicitis attack, and Dad told her, "Ruth, I'm going to pray for your healing. But if you do not have enough faith to get immediate results, then we are taking you to the doctor because a doctor can take care of this."

We need to realize that certain medical emergencies require immediate results. If immediate results are not forthcoming, then we need to go to the doctor so we can stay alive.

In the paper a few years ago, I read that some parents refused to take their nine-year-old boy to the doctor. The child had an appendicitis attack. His appendix finally burst and, of course, he died. That death was totally unnecessary, but sad to say, those parents thought they were believing God! They thought they were in faith.

Friends, in situations that are critical to your life, if a doctor can help you, go get some medical help! If your faith isn't producing immediate results and your life is in danger, go to a doctor!

Doctors and Proper Medication Do Not Hinder Faith

There is no reason that going to a doctor or using the proper medication should hinder your faith! In fact, the Bible tells you to *do* something—to take some positive action—to help yourself get well.

> **PROVERBS 18:9 (Amplified)**
> 9 . . . he who does not use **HIS ENDEAVORS TO HEAL HIMSELF** is brother to him who commits suicide.

One Tuesday afternoon in 1983, I sat in a room in the City of Faith hospital with four doctors who told me that my son, Craig, had a tumor on his brain about the size of a man's fist.

They informed me that the tumor was pressing against the brain stem and that the skull bone had become so thin across the area where that tumor had grown that the skull bone was as fragile as an egg shell. They said with any quick movement or bump to Craig's head, his skull could crack and shatter and he could die.

The doctors wanted to do surgery immediately. I said to them, "Just a minute" as I began to pray. Then I notified Dad and my wife, Lynette, and they both came up to the hospital.

I asked the doctors to give us two days to decide what to do. After two days, there were no immediate results, so we decided to go ahead with the surgery.

When we told the doctors that we'd decided to go ahead with the surgery, we were criticized by people who said, "Bless God! If that had been my son, I know what I would have done. I would just have believed God!"

But we did believe God! We prayed, and when we did not get immediate results, we all believed God for a perfect outcome from the surgery. As my dad often says, "When you don't get immediate results from your first line of defense, drop back to your second line of defense."

That's not a lack of faith! That's just using some wisdom. When people criticize me for allowing doctors to remove that tumor and save my son's life, I just look at them and say, "Well, it wasn't your son. *You* weren't in that position, so you really don't know what you would have done."

If you had prayed and believed God, but not seen any immediate results, what would you have done? If you needed an immediate manifestation and did not receive it, would you want to be the reason your child died—just so you could say you were "in faith"?

People can say what they want to, but they really don't know what they would do until they are in the same situation themselves.

And, actually, there was something I didn't know that affected the situation. Craig never talked about it much until years later when he spoke on a Christian television program. He said that after the tumor was removed, he realized that he was old enough when this happened that he should have used his own faith to be healed.

You see, there comes a time when children are old enough and spiritually mature enough to believe God for themselves. They can't continue to rely on their parents' faith any longer. In fact, there comes a time when parents can't carry their children on their faith anymore.

Anyway, Craig had the operation, which lasted twelve hours. The doctors were able to remove all of the tumor except just a little ridge. They explained that every time they tried to probe to get that last little ridge of the tumor, it caused problems that showed up on the brain-wave machine. Finally, they decided, "We're just going to leave it alone."

When the doctors couldn't remove all of the tumor, we stood in faith for Craig's complete recovery, and we received our answer from God. Craig was released, completely well! Not a thing was wrong with him. When Craig went back for his CAT scan, even that ridge was gone!

Normally, if this type of surgery is done when a child is a teenager, the skull bone does not grow back. But the doctors said they could see that the bone was growing back and the skull would be normal.

That entire incident was a life-threatening emergency that could be taken care of by medical science. It did not hinder my faith in God at all! In fact, we prayed and believed God, and the doctors said it was the most textbook-perfect operation of that kind they had ever experienced. In fact, the power of God was so strong in that operating room that one of the nurses was healed of a back problem!

People can criticize me all they want for allowing doctors to operate on my son, but Craig is with me today in the ministry, preaching the gospel of the Lord Jesus Christ. In fact, today Craig has a strong healing ministry. For example, the first fellow Craig ever prayed for was a blind man who was totally healed!

You can still have faith and use the benefits medical science has to offer. Medicine and doctors shouldn't negate your faith. Sometimes you may need to use medical science while you are exercising your faith to receive your complete healing. If that is the case, stay in faith. Take the medication in faith as you develop your faith in God's Word so you can receive your complete victory!

Chapter 3
Faith Is Not Neglect

And Jesus answering saith unto them, Have faith in God.

For verily I say unto you, That whosoever shall say unto this mountain, Be thou removed, and be thou cast into the sea; and shall not doubt in his heart, but shall believe that those things which he saith shall come to pass; he shall have whatsoever he saith.

Therefore I say unto you, What things soever ye desire, when ye pray, believe that ye receive them, and ye shall have them.

Mark 11:22–24

Now faith is the substance of things hoped for, the evidence of things not seen.

—Hebrews 11:1

Let's take another look at faith! Is faith a substitute for common sense and sound business practices? Is it an easy way out so believers don't have to work anymore? What does the Bible have to say about faith and practical matters such as finances and taking responsibility?

Some Christians actually believe that faith allows them to escape any responsibility to work or to handle finances wisely. Many people act like faith in God releases them from fulfilling all their responsibilities. But that's not scriptural!

Faith in God does not mean people can neglect their natural responsibilities and God will just take care of everything for them. Faith is not neglect! Faith is not some sort of substitute for a person's lack of responsibility! In other words, faith in God does not release people from their own responsibilities in life.

We live in a natural world where we must fulfill natural obligations as we trust and believe God to help us.

For example, some people say, "Well, I'm going to live by faith." Then they prop their feet up on the table, sit back and relax, thinking God will meet all their needs without any effort on their part. That's just irresponsible!

Believers cannot neglect their jobs or fail to pay their bills in the name of faith! Faith is not neglect.

What about faith for employment and finances? Sometimes there are steps you must take in the natural so you can receive what you're believing God for. Faith does not neglect the necessary steps of obedience that must be taken to receive from God.

For example, many people say, "I'm believing God for a job," but they neglect to go out and look for one. But normally no employer is going to beat down your door to ask you to go to work for him!

So after you pray and believe God, you must put some effort to looking for work! God will reward your effort. But how can a person say he is trusting God to meet his needs when all he does is sit around all day doing nothing!

If you want a job, and you are believing God for employment, then put some legs to your faith! Go out and start looking for a job! A person can't legitimately claim to be trusting God to meet his needs when he blatantly neglects what God's Word has to say about work.

In fact, we're told throughout the Word of God that if we walk in obedience to God, then whatever we put our hands to will prosper (Deut. 28:8). Joshua 1:7 also says that if we obey God and follow His ways, we will prosper.

Yes, believe God for financial blessings. Obey the principles in His Word about giving, and believe He will meet your needs. But then get up and put your hands to something! Don't just sit around saying, "Oh, Lord! Bring in the finances!"

Yes, God will prosper what we do, and He will prosper us for believing and acting on His Word. But believing and putting action to our faith work hand in hand.

You see, faith doesn't take the place of action. In other words, if you want a job, don't sit around your house doing nothing. Put your faith out for a good job, but then put some action to your faith and go out and look for work yourself.

God will come through for you because He promised to supply all your needs. But one of the ways He will supply is by *you* going to work to provide for yourself and your family (Phil. 4:19; 1 Tim. 5:8).

Pray and claim a good job based on God's Word. Then thank Him in faith: "Lord, I thank You that You are giving me a good job. I thank You for the job now when I pray. I believe I receive a good job, and I accept it now by faith."

Then you can tell people, "I'm believing God for my job." But if at ten o'clock Monday morning, you are still lying in bed, saying, "Thank You, Lord, for my job," you are not in faith.

Faith puts some action to prayer! If you are not going to take any action, you might as well say, "Twinkle, twinkle, little star. How I wonder what you are." Without any corresponding action to your prayers, that's all the good your prayers are doing.

If you are really believing God for a job, then get up and go out looking for work. Put action to your faith. Too many people use faith as a cop-out so they don't have to work. They don't want to work in the first place, so they make excuses by saying, "Lord, I thank You for a job," but never go look for one. Faith is not neglect!

What Did Paul Say About Work?

Actually, the Apostle Paul, the man who wrote more about faith than anyone else in the entire Word of God, is the one who wrote that if you don't work, you don't eat.

2 THESSALONIANS 3:10,11
10 For even when we were with you, this we commanded you, THAT IF ANY WOULD NOT WORK,

NEITHER SHOULD HE EAT.
11 For we hear that there are some which walk among you DISORDERLY, WORKING NOT AT ALL, but are busybodies.

Paul, the great man of faith, was a tentmaker by trade. In other words, Paul used his profession when necessary as he pioneered churches and visited works that he had established.

The Bible tells us about one offering that was finally taken up for him, and Paul was grateful for that (2 Cor. 1:11). And Paul taught that it is right to give material goods to those ministers who take care of the spiritual needs of others (1 Cor. 9:11).

When we read about Paul's faith exploits in the New Testament, we can see that he did more than just *talk* about a life of faith; he *lived* a life of faith. And even though Paul knew more about faith than anyone else, he did not just sit around doing nothing, expecting his faith to accomplish everything for him.

For instance, we never see Paul saying, "Since I'm living by faith, I don't have to do a thing!" Yes, Paul lived by faith, but he also used his faith by working in an area until his ministry was established there. He mixed some human effort with his faith!

The Bible says that people who don't work when they are able to work are walking "disorderly" (2 Thess. 3:11). They often become busybodies. For instance, I have noticed that many people who won't work because they are living by "faith" very often seem to run around sticking their nose into everyone else's business!

For some reason it seems that when we humans get hold of a new revelation from God's Word, we either run off into the ditch on the left side of the road or into the ditch on the right side of the road. One ditch is that believers can use their faith so they never have to work! The other ditch is when believers get so caught up in the work of the ministry that they get weary in well-doing (Gal. 6:9).

Now if you are in the ministry working for the Lord, you may not be working a secular job. You may be living entirely by faith. But in that case, you are not just sitting around doing nothing, expecting God to bring you food and money—you are actively involved in the work of the ministry.

Actually, the truth about God's prospering you is right down the middle of the road. God has His part to fulfill in prospering you, but *you* also have your part to fulfill so He *is able* to prosper you!

Some believers don't feel they need to do their part in providing for themselves and their families. Somehow they feel *they* are excluded from working for a living.

They say,"Lord, thank You for a job," and then sit at home and do nothing instead of going out to look for work.

Use Wisdom in Handling Finances

We need to use some common sense while we're believing God! I believe God to meet my needs, but I also have to work and be wise in handling my finances!

People who don't have any finances because they mismanage money often seem to be the very ones who go around telling others how to manage their money!

And have you ever noticed that the people who refuse to work are usually the very ones who are always going around telling others how to live their lives, raise their children, and how to manage their finances—when they don't have any money to manage themselves!

It's often the same way with some people who don't have children. Some of them seem to have great, grand ideas how other people should raise their children! But how can they know anything about it when they don't have any children themselves!

Besides, most parents start out raising their children with a lot of good ideas, but once their children actually begin growing and developing, they find out some of those ideas don't work. Raising children is a lot different than they thought!

A person needs to be wise in managing his own children and forget trying to manage other people's children! The same thing is true in finances. People need to be wise in managing their own finances and forget trying to manage everyone else's money.

Faith is not a substitute for common sense or for business sense! People cannot neglect their own finances by saying that God will take care of everything—and call that faith.

I believe God to meet my needs, but I also understand that if there is a change in the economy, I may have to budget my finances more closely.

Faith does not neglect natural responsibilities and common sense!

How many of you have lights at home so you can see to read your Bible? How many of you are comfortable in your homes because of heat or air-conditioning?

Well, the power company sends you a statement each month, and you have to pay the bill. If you don't pay it, one day you will be without lights and electricity. So it's your responsibility to pay your bills.

You can't just say, "Well, I believe God that those lights will stay on. Somehow I believe we'll just have heat in the wintertime," and then not pay your bills! You see, faith does not neglect responsibilities.

Some believers think that walking by faith means they can forget their responsibilities and every business principle they ever learned in life because they're believing God to meet their needs!

Yes, God will meet our needs. But He also expects us to do our part by working, budgeting our finances properly, and using some common sense. We can use the brains God gave us and still be in faith!

For example, if you know how to balance a budget and pay your bills on time, you can do what you know to do and still believe God for what you need. Using good business principles does not hinder faith.

Good, sound business principles dictate that you take responsibility for your own finances. For example, practically speaking, you shouldn't spend money you don't have. Wisely managing your money is just using wisdom.

The Bible tells us to be *". . . wise as serpents, and harmless as doves"* (Matt. 10:16). One translation uses the word "shrewd" instead of "wise." In other words, we are to be innocent and irreproachable in our business dealings, yet shrewd, wise, and sensible! Faith is not neglect.

Thank God, we can have faith and also be responsible. Exercising good common sense and some practical knowledge does not hinder faith. We can use the knowledge we have in the natural combined with the knowledge we have in the supernatural. As I stated earlier, there is a statement I've made for many years: "The natural and the supernatural coming together make an explosive force for God!"

There are certain biblical principles we must implement in our lives if we want to be successful. Faith is not neglecting the responsibilities of life. In fact, our faith in God will ensure that we fulfill our responsibilities in life. Actually, faith makes our natural responsibilities easier because we can believe God to help us.

For example, some people say, "God is going to meet my needs," but they don't ever bother to figure out that they spend more money than they take in. They aren't financially responsible, yet they say, "I'm believing God to supply all my needs." So am I, but I also use wisdom in handling my finances!

Faith is not meant to be used instead of good sense when it comes to handling finances. God is going to meet your needs if you continue to believe Him, but He also expects you to use some good practical sense.

It doesn't hurt to save financially. In fact, it's not always wise to spend everything you make. You need to be wise in finances. For example, David saved up a staggering amount of gold, which Solomon later used to build the temple for God (2 Sam. 8:11; 2 Chron. 5:1).

Faith Does Not Neglect To Plan

Faith does not take away your responsibility to plan and prepare. Have you ever met people who say they are living by faith but they never plan or prepare for anything? That's not faith; that's foolishness.

People like that always seem to get into trouble. God wants you to use your faith, but He also wants you to do some preparing and planning. Many people say, "But Jesus said to take no thought for tomorrow."

> **MATTHEW 6:34**
> **34 Take therefore no thought for the morrow: for the morrow shall take thought for the things of itself. Sufficient unto the day is the evil thereof.**

But if you will study the context, you will find out that Jesus was not talking against planning and preparation. He was talking about worrying. He was telling people to put their trust in God, not in their own plans and preparations.

That doesn't mean we shouldn't plan. It's good to plan for the future. Planning does not hinder faith. You can be in faith and still plan for the future. Just be sure you include God in your plans and allow Him to direct your future! Faith does not neglect the responsibility that is ours to plan and prepare.

> **PROVERBS 21:5 (NASB)**
> 5 The PLANS OF THE DILIGENT lead surely to advantage.

God's Word has a lot to say about being diligent. The word "diligent" means *work that is characterized by steady, earnest, and energetic effort*. God wants us to be diligent so we can enjoy every advantage in life. But He also wants us to include Him in our plans.

> **PROVERBS 10:4**
> 4 He becometh poor that dealeth with a slack hand: but the hand of the DILIGENT maketh rich.
> **PROVERBS 12:24**
> 24 The hand of the DILIGENT shall bear rule: but the slothful shall be under tribute.

Some people are diligent, but they fail to plan. Others plan, but they are not diligent, so their plans never come to pass.

You know, it's like the fellow who wanted to run to give a message to King David when David's army was fighting Absalom, David's rebellious son who staged an uprising against David.

David's commanders sent a runner to give David the message that the uprising against him had been subdued, but that David's son, Absalom, who had led the uprising, was dead (*see* Second Samuel chapter 18).

Another fellow standing nearby wanted to run to David just to be running. He didn't have the message, but he still wanted to run to David. He may have been diligent, but he had no plan of action because once he got to David, he didn't have anything to say!

He had no plan! When David saw that the runner had nothing to say, he told him, "Stand aside" (2 Sam. 18:30). You see, some believers are diligent; they want to do something for God, but they have no plan or purpose to fulfill that desire. So when the time comes when they should succeed, they have to stand aside because they haven't prepared properly—they have no plan.

Then there are others who have a plan, but they're not diligent enough to bring their plan to pass. God may have spoken to their heart about something He has for them to do, but if they put no effort to their God-given plan, they won't succeed.

Even when you have a plan, you've got to be diligent to work your plan. You can make plans and still be in faith. Just make sure that your confidence is always in God.

Faith vs. Insurance

What about faith versus insurance? Faith is not an insurance policy. Most states require car insurance. Some believers think they can refuse to get car insurance because they are standing in faith that they will never have an accident.

Believers who do that are in disobedience to God's Word, and God can't help them even though He wants to. Jesus Himself told His disciples, "Render unto Caesar that which is Caesar's" (Mark 12:17). When Jesus referred to Caesar, He was talking about the Roman state or the government.

At RHEMA, we require the training-center students to have car insurance before we give them a campus parking sticker because insurance is a requirement in this state. We are not going to be a party to breaking the law because then God can't bless us.

There's nothing wrong with having insurance. It shouldn't hinder a person's faith at all.

Some believers don't even make a will because they think faith automatically takes care of everything and they don't have any responsibility.

But if a person has young children, he has a responsibility to provide for them and to protect them (Prov. 13:22; 2 Cor. 12:14). One thing a will does is determine who will take care of the children should anything happen to the parents.

You say, "But I'm believing God that nothing bad is going to happen to me." I believe God for divine protection too. But believers still need to be wise in all the affairs of life.

Faith vs. Birth Control

What about faith and birth control? We laugh about this, but there are some people who are trying to use faith instead of birth-control measures. It won't work!

Several years ago, Dad and I were visiting a married couple who mentioned that they were using their faith as their birth-control method. Brother Hagin looked them right in the eyes and said, "That's foolish."

Anyway, their faith must have failed them because about ten months later they had a child! Don't try to use faith in areas where it doesn't apply.

We have all studied biology in school, and we've studied the physiological makeup of men and women. Therefore, it's foolish to try to go against natural laws that God Himself set into motion, saying, "Well, I'm just going to believe God to override this natural law."

But we need to realize that God created us the way we are. He created the process of child-bearing. He created the principle of seedtime and harvest. And He designed the way children come into this world.

God did not intend for us to use our faith as a birth-control measure. Natural laws work in that area. If married couples want to plan the size of their family, they should use other methods than faith for birth control. Faith was not designed to work in that area.

Regarding natural laws, we must do what we can do in the natural. We shouldn't be motivated by fear; we should be motivated by wisdom. We can still trust God but at the same time take our proper responsibilities in the natural realm.

Faith Is Not Imitation

It's important to understand that faith is not imitating someone else's actions! We can base our actions on the Word of God, but we cannot expect answers to prayers based on the testimonies of others—what other people *said* or *did*.

For example, I remember a person who gave his car away because God told him to do that, and someone gave him a much better car.

He received a car supernaturally by faith because he was in direct obedience to God when he gave his car away. But right after that some other believers also gave their cars away just based on that fellow's testimony. I noticed that several months later, they were still walking!

Why didn't their "faith" work for them? Because they based their faith on someone else's *actions*—not on the Word of God! They weren't believing God for themselves; they were just imitating what someone else had done. They said, "Well, that fellow gave his car away and got a new one, so that's what we're going to do too."

But, you see, the other person gave his car away in obedience to what God had told him to do. His faith was in God, and he based his giving on scriptural principles. These other people based their actions on imitating someone else's actions.

God will not meet you because you imitate what someone else did. God will meet you when you obey what He told *you* to do by His Spirit based on His Word. If you take action in obedience to God, you will prosper!

Sometimes God leads people in different ways, and as long as believers obey Him, they are blessed. But that does not mean they can just imitate what someone else did and expect to receive the same results. However, if they act on the Word of God, then they can expect the same results.

But some people act in "faith" just because they are imitating others. Their actions are not based on a personal faith in God; their actions are based on imitation.

Let me give you a biblical example of action that was based on imitation, not on faith in God. You'll notice that kind of action failed.

HEBREWS 11:29 (NIV)
29 By faith the people [the Israelites] **passed through the Red Sea as on dry land; but when the Egyptians tried to do so, they were drowned.**

The Egyptians tried to cross the Red Sea because they saw that the Israelites had successfully crossed it before them. But, you see, the Israelites were able to do the impossible—cross over the Red Sea on dry ground—because they were obeying God! When the Egyptians tried to imitate the Israelites' actions, that entire Egyptian army was drowned!

You can't step out in faith on someone's else's *actions*! However, if you see someone else's actions, and you search the Word for yourself, you can also respond to the promises in God's Word for yourself! Someone else's testimony can *inspire* your faith; but your actions must be based on your own faith in God's Word.

Many believers are acting in faith because that's what God's Word said to do: *"For therein is the righteousness of God revealed from faith to faith: as it is written, The just shall live by faith"* (Rom. 1:17). However, when people try to do something that is not based on their own faith and obedience but is only based on imitating someone else, they are acting like the Egyptians, and their efforts will fail!

You may have heard my testimony of my healing from an incurable fungal infection in my ear. Doctors said there was no medical cure; I'd just have to live with that condition and control it with medication. They also told me that I should never get that ear under water. I was in high school at the time, so that meant I could never participate in swimming in gym class.

But the Lord told me, "You are healed!" So in faith based on God's Word, "By My stripes you are healed" (1 Peter 2:24), and in obedience to the Holy Spirit, I jumped into the pool in gym class. When I dove underwater, I heard a popping sound in my ear. My ear popped open, and I knew I was totally healed!

But I don't tell everyone to do what I did. For me, jumping in that pool in obedience to God's Word was the action I felt in my heart I needed to take to demonstrate my faith—but I'd already heard the Lord speak to me.

Therefore, I was healed based on my own faith in God's Word *as I obeyed the Lord*. But I don't go around advising everyone with an ear infection to jump into a swimming pool to get healed of their ear infections!

And just because one preacher who had sugar diabetes threw away his insulin is no sign that if you have sugar diabetes, you should throw your medication away. That's dangerous!

Remember, every time that preacher gave himself a shot of insulin, he said, "I thank You, God, that You are working in my body to effect a healing and a cure."

But he kept right on taking his medicine believing that God was working in the situation. But the day came when he didn't need his insulin anymore because he was totally healed, so he threw it away.

In another example, a man also believed God's Word concerning healing. But because of the particular way God impressed him, he threw away his medicine and was healed too. Without being specifically led of the Lord, wisdom lets you know that you can only follow the first example. In both cases, healing ultimately came to the men because of their faith in God's Word.

To receive from God, each person must act in faith based on the Word for himself—not based on someone else's action.

I don't recommend that people with incurable ear infections do what I did. For example, if someone with an ear infection followed my actions, threw his medicine away and jumped into a swimming pool, he could get in trouble if he's not in faith. If he was just imitating my actions, and his faith wasn't based on the Word, he probably wouldn't be healed.

I recommend that people believe God's Word for themselves and put the Word of God in their heart so that they know exactly how to act in faith.

HEBREWS 13:7 (NIV)
7   Remember your leaders, who spoke the word

of God to you. Consider the outcome of THEIR WAY OF LIFE and IMITATE THEIR FAITH. . . .

You see, the Bible doesn't say to imitate other people's way of life. In other words, it doesn't say to imitate people's *actions*; it says to imitate their *faith*.

There is a difference between imitating someone's action or lifestyle, and imitating someone's faith. You can imitate someone's lifestyle and not have one ounce of faith. That's why we can follow someone else's *faith* that's based on the Word of God, but not someone else's *actions*. We can follow scriptural faith, not what someone else says or does.

The Bible says that we are to remember our leaders who spoke the Word of God to us. We are to consider the outcome of their way of life and imitate their faith. I like this verse because it shows us that we are to be actively involved in believing God for ourselves, not just imitating someone else.

I remember back in the early '70s, the message of faith was just taking off on a large scale. Someone would give a good testimony, telling how God had blessed him, and you would hear other people say, "Well, I claim that same blessing too!"

Claiming God's blessings based on someone else's experience rather than on the Word of God caused a lot of confusion in the Body of Christ back then. When believers didn't receive what they claimed, they couldn't understand why. But it was because they didn't base their petition on the solid foundation of God's Word.

I remember that during that time, Brother Hagin was teaching people to base their faith on the Word. He told them, "You can't say, 'I claim that blessing!' just because someone else received it. Faith doesn't work that way! Nowhere in the Bible does it say to base your faith on someone's testimony. You have to claim your petition based on your faith in God's Word. Then the promises of God will work for you like they worked for others."

People were giving their testimony saying, "God gave me a car." Or "God gave me a house." Other people heard that and began saying, "I claim one too!"

But it didn't work, because they were imitating someone else's actions! They had never taken time to develop their own faith in the Word. They had never taken the time to get the promises of God deeply rooted in their own hearts. Their confession was based on what someone else had received, not on the Word of God.

We are not to be imitators of someone else's action. We are to develop faith in the Word of God for ourselves. We are to go to God and claim what belongs to us in Christ based on God's promise to us.

Build your faith confessions on the promises in God's Word:

> I am more than a conqueror in Christ. My God will supply all of my needs according to His riches in glory by Christ Jesus. It is my Father's good pleasure to give me the Kingdom, and my Father always gives me the victory through my Lord

Jesus Christ. (Rom. 8:37; Phil. 4:19; Luke 12:32;
1 Cor. 15:57).

Start exercising your faith! Find scriptures in God's
Word that promise you what you need. Then stand
steadfastly on the Word. Diligently claim God's promises
to you, and you will see God meet your every need!

Chapter 4
Faith Is Not a Formula

And Jesus answering saith unto them, Have faith in God.

For verily I say unto you, That whosoever shall say unto this mountain, Be thou removed, and be thou cast into the sea; and shall not doubt in his heart, but shall believe that those things which he saith shall come to pass; he shall have whatsoever he saith.

Therefore I say unto you, What things soever ye desire, when ye pray, believe that ye receive them, and ye shall have them.

—Mark 11:22–24

Now faith is the substance of things hoped for, the evidence of things not seen.

—Hebrews 11:1

Let's take another look at faith! Bible faith is not a legalistic formula. It seems that so many people have tried to relegate faith to seven principles or to twelve steps. Now it is true that there are certain principles of faith. And when we teach faith, we often refer to various biblical principles that work together to help activate our faith.

But on the other hand, faith is not a set of legalistic formulas. Yes, some basic *principles* of faith operate together to cause faith to work. For example, in Mark 11:23, we find two basic faith principles that work together. One is *believing* God. The second principle is *saying or confessing* what we believe based on God's Word.

> **MARK 11:23,24**
> **23 For verily I say unto you, That whosoever shall SAY unto this mountain, Be thou removed, and be thou cast into the sea; and shall not doubt in his heart, but shall believe that those things which he saith shall come to pass; he shall have whatsoever he saith.**
> **24 Therefore I say unto you, What things soever ye desire, when ye pray, believe that ye receive them, and ye shall have them.**

So there are scriptural principles that govern faith, but we need to be careful that we don't get hung up on formulas. According to the dictionary, a "formula" can be *a set of words used by ritual or rote.* God doesn't respond to formulas, but He does respond to faith in His Word (Isa. 55:11; Ps. 138:2; Heb. 11:6).

Many people have overemphasized the part that confession plays in faith by turning it into a legalistic formula. Then faith becomes nothing more than a mental exercise. But Bible faith originates in man's heart—in his recreated spirit. And Bible faith is what gets the job done, not some mental exercise!

People can get so involved in confession that they lose sight of the other principles that work with faith to make it effective such as: love, patience, hope, and perseverance. People can begin making strong confessions, but without these other spiritual qualities activating faith, their faith can become weak and inoperative.

Then they wonder why their faith won't work! So they try to make their faith confessions come to pass in their own strength, and they end up saying, "This faith business doesn't work!"

But when your faith is energized by the love of God, plus hope, patience, and perseverance—your faith will work!

So many believers have become obsessed with faith formulas instead of Bible faith that is empowered by these other spiritual qualities! For instance, some believers think that if they confess something 5,000 times, it has to come to pass! That's just not so!

Confessions that are not based on the Word will not come to pass just because you confess them. But, faith confessions based on God's Word *will* produce results.

ISAIAH 55:11
11 So shall my word be that goeth forth out of my mouth: it shall not return unto me void, but it shall accomplish that which I please, and it shall prosper in the thing whereto I sent it.

God promises that His Word won't go out and come back void, but it will "*. . . prosper in the thing whereto I sent it.*" So you can see that there is quite a difference between just confessing words and confessing *the* Word!

MATTHEW 24:35
35 Heaven and earth shall pass away, but my
words shall not pass away.

When people do things by rote using formulas, they
miss the spirit of faith. When I tell some people they're
missing the spirit of faith with their faith formulas,
they tell me, "Oh, don't confess that!" But I'm not making a *confession* at all—I'm just stating a *fact.* There is
a big difference between making a faith confession and
stating facts.

Sometimes believers can be so bound up in fear
about confession that a person can't seem to say anything. For example, have you ever walked into a room
and just simply made a casual statement, and everyone
jumped on you for making a bad confession? One time I
walked into an auditorium where two fellows I knew
were working on the church sound equipment.

I knew them well, so I was just kidding when I
said, "With those two fellows working on the sound
equipment, it may never work!"

One of the men in charge said with fear in his voice,
"Oh! Don't confess that!"

I answered, "What in the world are you talking
about? I was only joking."

Sometimes believers are so fearful about confession,
a person can't say anything around them! Every time
you open your mouth, they answer, "Oh! Don't confess
that! It might come to pass!"

When people respond to casual remarks by saying,
"Don't make that bad confession!" I try to show them

the difference between bad confessions and casual remarks.

It's important that people see the difference between a casual remark that comes from your *head* and a faith statement based on the Word that comes from your *heart*.

Ritual or Faith?

Yes, it is scriptural to make daily faith confessions based on the Word of God. But I have a problem when people make daily confessions just by rote and ritual. When confessions simply become a ritualistic mental formula, they become ineffectual.

"Are you saying we shouldn't make faith confessions?" you may ask. No, I'm not saying that. But I am saying that faith confessions shouldn't become a ritualistic formula. When faith confessions get ritualistic, they become unproductive.

Do you remember the "precious promise box" that were especially popular in the '50s and early '60s? Some believers would pull a promise out of the promise box instead of reading the Word of God! And some people tried to live their lives based just on those little promises.

But that won't work because we need the whole counsel of God! And we each need to get the Word of God into our hearts for ourselves. Grabbing a "promise" as you rush out the door to work becomes nothing more than a ritual.

In most cases, it was just something some believers did every day as a ritualistic habit. It had nothing to do with worshipping God or edifying and building up the spiritual man.

Well, ritualistic faith confessions become little more than grabbing a promise out of the promise box—they lose their meaning. There is nothing wrong with making faith confessions, but let's just make sure that our confessions are based on God's Word. Also, let's make sure our faith confessions come from a heart of worshipping God, not based on ritualistic formulas.

There's quite a difference between doing something ritualistically, and doing something because you are earnestly seeking God. You just can't afford to allow faith to be reduced to legalistic formulas!

Faith Is Not Ordering God Around

Faith is also not a matter of manipulating God or ordering Him around. Have you ever heard people say, "Oh, those faith people are detracting from the sovereignty of God because they are always using their faith to order God around!"

But are you ordering someone around by simply asking for something the person has already promised you?

In the natural, are your children ordering you around when they ask you for something you promised them? For example, suppose you tell your children, "If you make good grades, I will do such and such for you."

When your children receive their grades and meet all your conditions, are they ordering you around when they remind you of your promise? Are they manipulating you when they ask you for what you told them was theirs? No, they are simply claiming your promise to them!

It is the same principle spiritually. When we stand on God's Word, we are simply going to God with His promises. We are simply reminding God of His Word and asking Him to give us what belongs to us. We are doing what God told us to do. In fact, in His Word, God invited us to remind Him of His promises.

ISAIAH 43:26
26 Put me in remembrance: let us plead together: declare thou, that thou mayest be justified.

It is scriptural for a believer to take his stand on the Word of God and remind God what He has promised in His Word. In fact, God said to put Him in remembrance of His Word and what He has promised us.

You see, faith believes what God has already *said*; faith responds to what God has already *done*; and faith receives what God has already *provided*.

It is not arrogant for a child to remind his parents of a promise made to him. That's not arrogance, disobedience, manipulation, or disrespect. It is simply asking for what was already promised.

Therefore, it is not arrogant for us to ask our Heavenly Father for the gifts or benefits He already provided for us. We are just claiming in faith what He has promised in His Word. It does not detract from God's sovereignty to put Him in remembrance of His Word!

Taking a stand on God's Word is not arrogant! And when you stand on God's Word against the devil, you can't be mealy-mouthed and wishy-washy about it! You must know who you are in Christ and take your authority over the devil.

You've got to be strong in the Lord! You've got to boldly declare who you are in Christ. That's not arrogance—that's faith! When we are bold in Christ, we are not taking an arrogant stance against *God*. We are taking a strong stance against the problem and against our enemy, Satan, based on the authority of God's Word (Luke 10:19; Phil. 2:9,10).

Let the devil know you are not going to be intimidated by him or his devices. That's not arrogance against God; that's acting boldly in your authority over the devil. It's boldly standing in your place of authority because the Word said that Jesus defeated the devil. And because Satan has been defeated, *you* can be bold as a lion.

PROVERBS 28:1
1 The wicked flee when no man pursueth: BUT THE RIGHTEOUS ARE BOLD AS A LION.

You are dealing with a defeated foe that is already under your feet because he's under Jesus' feet, so you can be bold in your authority! The devil has already been defeated by the Lord Jesus Christ!

Jesus said, ". . . *All power is given unto me in heaven and in earth*" (Matt. 28:18). Then He said, "Go ye," giving that power to His Church on the earth (Matt. 28:19).

So why should we be weak and afraid to deal with a defeated foe—when we have the authority in Jesus' Name to put him in his place?

It is not arrogant to scripturally come against the enemy that is trying to steal from us what God has already given us. When you know God's Word, you get bold and strong in the Lord!

But when people don't really know what God's Word says, they don't have the boldness to stand against the devil. And some believers only know what someone *thought* God's Word said. But if they would study the Word for themselves, they would see for themselves that *they* have authority over the devil in Jesus' Name!

Some believers aren't sure about their authority in Christ because they are still trying to figure out everything in their natural minds. They say, "This is how I *interpret* this scripture." Or "This is what I *think* this scripture means."

Then they try to explain away the truth of God's Word theologically because it doesn't coincide with what they believe, and they can't figure it out with their natural mind (1 Cor. 2:14).

But when you are dealing with faith, you can't always figure out the way God works with your natural mind. Faith does not always make sense. It is not always logical, and you can't always understand spiritual things mentally. But as long as you walk in obedience to God, you can claim and receive what His Word says belongs to you.

You see, boldness rises up on the inside of you when you know God's Word. When you find out who you are in Christ, what you are in Christ, and what belongs to you because of Jesus' redemption at Calvary, then you can boldly proclaim what the Word says.

Don't mistake boldness for arrogance. We aren't supposed to be arrogant. But on the other hand, refuse to be intimidated by those who teach contrary to the Word of God. When I know what God's Word says about something, I refuse to back down. Why? Because God said it. And if God said it, I can have it, and I'm going to boldly declare it!

That's not arrogance—that just bold faith! I'm going to take God at His Word and enjoy my Christian life before I go to Heaven. God said we don't have to wait until we go to Heaven before we are victorious in our Christian walk. His Word said we can be victors in *this* life!

Some believers live their whole lives just waiting to go to Heaven. They say, "Oh, some happy day, it will all be over, and then we'll be in Heaven!"

I thank God for that day when we will go to Heaven—to that city with streets of gold! But the Word of God also tells me that I do not have to be under the devil's dominion while I'm living down here on this earth! The Bible tells me that I can live a life of happiness, joy, and peace right here on earth. I don't have to be poor or sick anymore.

And I'm going to be bold and declare what the Bible says I have in Christ! It's time to take a strong stand on God's Word! Are there areas in your life where the devil is trying to steal, kill, and destroy (John 10:10)? Then take a bold stand against the devil with the Word! He's under your feet! It doesn't matter what *people* say—it matters what God's *Word* says!

And when I find out what God's Word says about any subject, then I know that is God's will. I'm going to claim God's will for my life and walk in it! And I'm going to enjoy the triumph in every circumstance because God promises me the victory!

1 CORINTHIANS 15:57
57 But thanks be to God, which giveth us the victory through our Lord Jesus Christ.

I've got the victory now! No more bondage in Jesus' Name. For sickness, I have health. For poverty, wealth—since Jesus set me free!

Whatever you need, receive it from the Word of God. Boldly declare the Word over your circumstances! Boldly declare your faith, whether you can see your answer, feel it, or taste it! Take it by faith!

You see, when you base your faith on God's Word, you can say, "It's mine! I have my answer now!" How can you be that bold in your faith declaration? Because Jesus already made provision for your every need to be met. That's why you can receive your answer in faith when you pray (Mark 11:24).

Grab hold of God's Word with the tenacity of a bulldog with a bone. Don't let go of His Word! Tenaciously hold on to God's promises. That's when you receive results!

I have two dogs named Princess and Dottie. Princess is a black lab and Dottie is a dalmatian. When I go to the back door with bones in my hand, those dogs sit there and wait patiently until I tell them they can have the bones. I've trained them to do that.

But as soon as I say, "Okay!" those dogs grab those bones and don't let go! Once they get hold of those bones, I don't try to take them away, because they hold on to them with the tenacity of a bulldog.

That's the way believers need to be about the promises of God. Get the Word of God down in your heart, and hold on to the Word! The Word is more powerful than your circumstances or anything you could ever face in this life!

If I tried to grab hold of those bones, those dogs would just tighten their grip! That's what you need to do when the devil tries to steal your blessings away from you. Tighten your faith grip on God's promises! Don't let loose of the Word! Tell the devil, "In the Name of Jesus, stop in your maneuvers against me!"

Some of you just need to get in faith and laugh at the devil because you have victory over him. Break free of the devil's lies by shouting your victory in faith because God's Word is true and you receive your answer now!

Do whatever *you* need to do to demonstrate your faith in God's Word. Strengthen your faith so you can walk in the freedom Jesus already purchased for you! You don't have to receive anything the devil tries to throw at you because he's a defeated foe!

Sometimes believers will receive something from God in church where the corporate anointing is strong.

But when they get out there in their everyday lives by themselves, the first time the devil tries to take their blessing away from them, they back down in fear and let him have it.

But you have to be strong in the Lord and hold fast to what belongs to you in Christ! You need to praise the Lord for your victory before you see the answer (Mark 11:24). If someone asks you, "Why are you carrying on like that?" tell them, "Because I've got the victory!"

In sports events, when a team wins the championship, people dance in the streets; they jump, laugh, and carry on. They show some emotion! But when God does something for us and we rejoice in Him, some people want to call us fanatics!

Let them call us fanatics if they want to! Glory to God! The Bible says it; I believe it; and it's His Word that sets me free! When you receive your petition from the Lord, you rejoice in Him!

The Bible says, *"Make a joyful noise unto the Lord, all the earth: make a loud noise, and rejoice, and sing praise"* (Ps. 98:4). It also says that we are to enter into His gates with thanksgiving, and into His courts with praise! We are to be thankful to Him, and bless His holy Name (Ps. 100:4).

So we can rejoice in our victory by faith before we see our answer because we know God is faithful! Victory is ours! Don't ever let the devil take anything away from you. You may have to stand your ground on God's Word to ensure your victory, but be strong in the Lord and tell the devil, "Flee, in the Name of Jesus!"

Every time you take your authority over the devil in the Name of Jesus, it's like giving the devil a black eye spiritually. Every time you are bold in your authority in Jesus, it's like giving the devil a left hook to the jaw spiritually. It puts him in his place! When you stand on your authority in Christ, the devil has to flee!

If the devil is walking all over you, maybe it's because you haven't stood up to him in your authority in Christ. Put him in his place with the Word of God. If you are in Christ, the Bible says the devil is under your feet because he's under Jesus' feet! So put the devil on the run with the Name of Jesus!

Rejoice in the Lord because Jesus is your victory! It doesn't matter whether you feel like it or not. It doesn't matter what your mind is saying to you if it's contrary to the Word of God. Rejoice in the Lord because His Word promises you the victory! Thank God, His Word never fails. You can be bold and confess what God says about you and receive your answer now!

Chapter 5
Faith Is Not a Ticket to Utopia

And Jesus answering saith unto them, Have faith in God.

For verily I say unto you, That whosoever shall say unto this mountain, Be thou removed, and be thou cast into the sea; and shall not doubt in his heart, but shall believe that those things which he saith shall come to pass; he shall have whatsoever he saith.

Therefore I say unto you, What things soever ye desire, when ye pray, believe that ye receive them, and ye shall have them

—Mark 11:22–24

Now faith is the substance of things hoped for, the evidence of things not seen.

—Hebrews 11:1

Let's take another look at faith! Some people have the idea that if you have faith, you'll never experience any more problems in life. They think that if a person just has enough faith in God, life will be perfect and everything will go smoothly all the time. But that's not what the Bible teaches!

Faith in God does not produce a continual state of Utopia. What is Utopia? Actually, it was an imaginary place in literature where everything was perfect—society, politics, and law. Now we use the word "Utopia" in our own language to mean a place of ideal perfection.

Faith in God does not produce a state of Utopia—a condition of perpetual bliss. In other words, just because you are believing God, that's no sign you are going to float through life on flowery beds of ease. Many people get the idea that once they begin to live by faith, God will just automatically do everything for them.

But it is unrealistic and unbiblical to expect faith to be a ticket to Utopia, because the Word of God says we are going to have tests and trials in this life. But it also says, "My God has delivered us out of them all!" Faith in God is knowing He will deliver us out of all our tests and trials.

The Word of God says God will bless what you put your hand to (Deut. 28:8). And God also says in His Word that we can receive the victory in every situation (2 Cor. 2:14). But it is very unrealistic and unbiblical to think that you can believe God to never have another problem in life. If you have that idea, somehow you are not reading the Scripture correctly. The Bible doesn't say that!

PSALM 34:19
19 Many are the afflictions of the righteous: but the LORD delivereth him out of them all.

The Bible tells us exactly why we suffer affliction and persecution in this life! It's for the Word's sake.

Jesus Himself said that in this world, we would suffer persecution.

> **MARK 4:17**
> **17 . . . when affliction or persecution ariseth for the word's sake. . . .**
>
> **JOHN 16:33**
> **33 These things I have spoken unto you, that in me ye might have peace. In the world ye shall have tribulation: but be of good cheer; I have overcome the world.**

We are still in this world! I realize we've been born again, and we belong to the family of God. But in the natural, we are still living in this world. And Jesus said, "In this world, you *shall* have tribulation."

Many people don't like to hear that because it makes them face the fact that they have to take some responsibility in this life. Many people just want to say, "Well, I'm believing God, so He'll take care of everything," and then they don't make any effort to do their part to receive from God. They don't understand there are things *they* must do to receive the blessings of God.

It is utterly ridiculous for people of faith to ignore the facts and deny their responsibilities in life just because they say, "Well, I'm just going to live by faith." Some believers seem to think they can surround themselves in some kind of faith "cocoon" and never be affected by this world that the rest of us have to deal with.

But, friend, we still live in the natural world! Yes, our citizenship is in Heaven, but we also still have natural citizenship. And in the natural, we must deal with natural problems.

Problems will always exist in the natural realm as long as we live on this earth. No matter how much faith you have or how much of the Word of God you can quote, as long as you are in this world, you will still experience some trials and tribulations from time to time.

> **ACTS: 14:21,22**
> **21 And when they had preached the gospel to that city, and had taught many, they returned again to Lystra, and to Iconium, and Antioch,**
> **22 Confirming the souls of the disciples, and exhorting them to continue in the faith, and that we must through much tribulation enter into the kingdom of God.**

Now it's true that we can use our faith in God's Word to deal with problems that we face on this earth and overcome them. We don't have to be overcome by problems. Empowered with God's Word, the Word can overcome any problem!

Fight the Good Fight of Faith

Name any hero of faith in the Word of God, and I will show you a strong man or woman of faith who overcame obstacles, challenges, tests, and trials! For example, look at Paul's life. He suffered some tests and trials!

> **2 CORINTHIANS 11:23–28**
> **23 Are they ministers of Christ? (I speak as a fool) I am more; in labours more abundant, in stripes**

above measure, in prisons more frequent, in deaths oft.
24 Of the Jews five times received I forty stripes save one.
25 Thrice was I beaten with rods, once was I stoned, thrice I suffered shipwreck, a night and a day I have been in the deep;
26 In journeyings often, in perils of waters, in perils of robbers, in perils by mine own countrymen, in perils by the heathen, in perils in the city, in perils in the wilderness, in perils in the sea, in perils among false brethren;
27 In weariness and painfulness, in watchings often, in hunger and thirst, in fastings often, in cold and nakedness.
28 Beside those things that are without, that which cometh upon me daily, the care of all the churches.

Paul said he'd been beaten, left for dead, thrown in jail, in peril in the sea, stoned and left for dead. But in all of the trials Paul endured, he kept on believing God. His faith in God never wavered. In fact, he went on later to say, "I am always victorious in Christ Jesus."

Paul, that great man of faith who wrote more about faith than anyone else in the New Testament, suffered some trials and tribulations on this earth! But he was victorious because he understood that his trials and tribulations were not the final chapter in his walk of faith. He knew his faith in God would see him through everything he suffered so he would come out the victor.

That great apostle of faith, Smith Wigglesworth, once said, "Great victories come out of great battles."

That is scriptural because each one of us will fight the good fight of faith from time to time in the circumstances of life.

1 TIMOTHY 6:12
12 Fight the good fight of faith, lay hold on eternal life, whereunto thou art also called, and hast professed a good profession before many witnesses.

Everyone wants victory in life, but friend, the only way you'll ever receive victory is to fight the good fight of faith! If there is no fight of faith, there will be no victory! Before you can enjoy the victory, you've got to enter into the arena of faith in God's Word because Satan will try to oppose you—but he's no match for the Word!

For example, in the natural, just because you enter an athletic field of competition dressed in the proper equipment, that does not automatically secure you the victory. No, you have to get on the field of competition and defeat the opposing team!

But, thank God, we can equip ourselves with the full armor of God, and armed with the Word of God, we can expect the victory before we ever get to the battlefield! Why? Because the Lord Jesus Christ has already given us the victory!

We need to claim what belongs to us! Jesus already defeated Satan for us. Jesus has given us His armor, His Name, and His Word. We just need to learn to wear our spiritual equipment properly so we are ready for the fight of faith.

For example, it would do a football player no good to put his helmet on backwards. It would still be a football helmet, and it would still protect his head. But if he wears it backwards, he wouldn't be able to see where he's going. He couldn't even see the action on the field!

It's the same way spiritually. Once you are wearing your spiritual equipment—the armor of God—you still have to use your equipment properly before you can succeed.

EPHESIANS 6:11–17
11 Put on THE WHOLE ARMOUR OF GOD, that ye may be able to stand against the wiles of the devil.
12 For we wrestle not against flesh and blood, but against principalities, against powers, against the rulers of the darkness of this world, against spiritual wickedness in high places.
13 Wherefore take unto you THE WHOLE ARMOUR OF GOD, that ye may be able to withstand in the evil day, and having done all, to stand.
14 Stand therefore, having your LOINS GIRT ABOUT WITH TRUTH, and having on THE BREASTPLATE OF RIGHTEOUSNESS;
15 And your FEET SHOD WITH THE PREPARATION OF THE GOSPEL OF PEACE;
16 Above all, taking THE SHIELD OF FAITH, wherewith ye shall be able to quench all the fiery darts of the wicked.
17 And take the HELMET OF SALVATION, and the SWORD OF THE SPIRIT, which is the word of God.

In a baseball game, the catcher wears a padded chest protector. It would be foolish for him to put that chest protector on his back and go out on the field to play ball. He also wears a face mask, but if he puts it on backwards, the back of his head is protected, but his face is exposed. You see, he would be wearing the right equipment, but he would be wearing it improperly.

Many people have put on the helmet of salvation, but they have not bothered to use the other pieces of their spiritual equipment: the breastplate of righteousness, the shield of faith, the shoes of peace, the sword of the Spirit, and the belt of truth. If they don't wear their equipment properly, they are vulnerable to the enemy.

For example, it is the shield of faith that quenches all the fiery darts of the enemy. Notice that as you live your life for God on this earth claiming God's promises, the enemy will shoot his fiery darts at you. But even though he tries to oppose you, your shield of faith in God's Word will overcome every one of his fiery darts. With your faith shield held high, you can keep those fiery darts from hurting you.

Don't Relax Your Guard

It doesn't matter how heavy that shield of faith gets, you've got to keep it up! If you don't use your faith as a shield, sooner or later you will get into trouble spiritually. So don't let your shield of faith sag in doubt and unbelief! Don't relax your guard spiritually!

Have you ever noticed that a boxer keeps his hands up in front of his face for protection. He keeps his elbows tucked in at his side to protect his body, and his head hunched down to protect his neck.

When his opponent tries to hit him in the stomach, he can use his elbows to ward off the blows. His hands in front of his face are an effective protection to help deflect any blows his opponent throws at him.

When I was a junior in high school, we were required to take boxing in gym class. We wore huge, padded gloves so we wouldn't hurt anyone. Actually, they were so padded, they were like pillows tied on our hands.

At first, I wasn't used to holding my arms up in front of my face for protection, so I'd get tired and drop my arms. But I soon found out that once I dropped my guard, I was an open target for my opponent.

Sometimes in a boxing match, if a boxer is winning, he may relax his guard a little and without thinking, drop his hands down. That leaves him unprotected and wide open so his opponent can tag him right on the chin.

That's what many believers are doing spiritually. They are living by faith in God's Word and everything is going smoothly. But when things are going well, they relax their guard and let their shield of faith down, and Satan nails them.

They were wielding the shield of faith and staying in victory, but then they got careless and thought, *I can relax for a while.* Then "BOOM!" the enemy hit them with a test or a trial.

Walking with God in faith does not guarantee that you won't ever have tests and trials! But as long as you keep your faith shield held high, believing, trusting, and walking in God's Word, you are guaranteed that God will see you through to victory. Jesus always causes you to triumph in Him!

Faith Is Not a Panic Button

Some people have thought that faith was just a panic button to push in the event of a crisis. For example, in the Old Testament we see that many times the Israelites pushed the panic button when they got into trouble with their enemies.

The Israelites seemed to operate this way all the time. As long as everything was going well, they didn't have time for God. But as soon as they got into trouble, they ran crying to God. When the crises of life came, they cried out to God, "Lord, deliver us!"

We do the same thing spiritually. When things go well, we may not be seeking God as diligently as we should. But the minute a crisis comes our way, we run to God. But God doesn't want us to live from crisis to crisis and from panic to panic. He wants us to trust Him all the time!

HABAKKUK 2:4
4　... the just shall live by his faith.

The scripture "the just shall live by faith" means that faith is to be a lifestyle for the Christian. Faith as a lifestyle means you walk by your faith in God every day of your life, 365 days a year, regardless of circumstances!

Faith becomes a way of life, not a panic button you push every time you get into trouble.

God doesn't intend for faith to be something you just use in the crises of life. Faith is something you must use every day of the week if you are going to walk with God. God wants you to trust Him every day for the little things as well as for the big things. He wants you to lean and rely on Him continually. You are to claim His promises for your life daily, not just when the going gets tough.

In fact, if you wait till the crisis comes to try to believe God, you've waited too late. You need God's Word in your heart before the crisis ever happens. You need to meditate on God's Word continually to get it into your heart.

If you've ever been involved in an exercise program, you know what happens if you miss several weeks and then start exercising again. You can't start out at the same exercise level as you were when you quit. You get tired faster because you are no longer in the same physical shape you were before. You have to build your endurance back up to the level you were at physically before you quit exercising.

Exercise is something you have to do all the time for it to really profit you. A life of faith in God works the same way. There will never be a time you can quit using your faith and just relax and take it easy. The day you relax and quit exercising your faith is the day you quit progressing in your Christian walk.

No, you must keep your faith strong and alive until the day Jesus Christ comes to take us home to Heaven. Until then, you need to continually exercise your faith because the devil is just waiting to try to take you unawares. He's waiting for the day you lower your shield of faith and relax your grip on the Word. Then "Wham!" he will hit you with a fiery dart.

The Bible says Satan is going around as a roaring lion seeking whom he may devour (1 Peter 5:8). That means we don't need to be devoured! Well, how do we keep from being devoured? By continually using our faith, not as a crutch in a crisis situation, but as a strong shield to protect us from the enemy.

Faith as a shield means that I walk with God every day. Daily I believe God and obey His Word. I continually surround myself with God's promises. Armed with the Word, I shield myself from the enemy.

PSALM 23:4
4   Yea, though I walk through the valley of the shadow of death, I will fear no evil: for thou art with me; thy rod and thy staff they comfort me.

The Bible says we can walk through the valley of the shadow of death but fear no evil. When you've been living faith, confessing faith, and surrounding yourself with faith from the Word, you can walk through the very midst of the pits of hell, and the power of the enemy will have no effect on you.

Faith is not something we just use when we're in a crisis! It's not a panic button we push in the storms of life.

We need strong faith in God every day of the week. Wrap yourself in the promises of God, and you'll experience the peace of God in every situation!

As God's children, we have been blessed with all spiritual blessings in heavenly places (Eph. 1:3). We are seated with Christ now (Eph. 2:6). In that sense, we are shielded from hard times. Yes, in the natural we do run into some hard times—the tests, trials, and tribulations we all go through in life.

But, thank God, we are seated with Christ in heavenly places! So when our natural eyes see nothing but dark disappointment and bleak despair all around us, with the eye of faith we can see the golden glow of God's power coming to our rescue on the horizon! As we fix our eyes on the light of God's Word, by faith we can walk out of any dark situation into the delivering power of God!

But you must take those steps of faith to walk from dark circumstances into the light of God's Word. God has already provided for your complete victory in every situation. But you must lift up your shield of faith like a banner of victory by proclaiming the power of God's Word! With your head held high, walk in your triumph in Christ!

Faith Is Not a Magic Wand

Faith is not some kind of magic wand you wave around to get what you want in God. The Bible is not a magic lamp you can rub so a genie will pop out to grant you three wishes. Some believers seem to think faith works like that. It is unfortunate that some people have heard a few faith principles and then tried to use them for materialistic gain.

PSALM 119:105
105 Thy word is a lamp unto my feet, and a light unto my path.

Yes, the Bible is a lamp to light our paths so we can see where we are going in life spiritually. And by faith we take one step at a time on the path that God has for us. Usually that's about as much light as the Lord will shed on our pathway because He expects us to walk by faith, not by sight.

I remember in drivers' education in high school, the instructors talked about night driving and said, "Don't overdrive your lights." What did they mean by that statement? They meant don't go any faster than the time it takes for you to stop within the distance that your headlights are shining. The headlights of your car only extend so far, so allow yourself at least that much distance to stop.

The same thing is true spiritually. We could say it this way: Don't go beyond the light of God's Word. Don't walk out beyond the light that God's Word has shone on your path.

The Bible is a light, not a magic wand that we wave over negative situations. The Word of God is a light so we can find the paths that God wants us to walk on. As a light, it dispels darkness because where the glorious light of the gospel shines, there is no darkness. When we're not groping around in the darkness, it's much easier to know where we are going!

If you turned out all the lights in a room, you could light one candle, and wherever that light shines, darkness is dispelled. Darkness cannot overpower light, but light extinguishes darkness. Darkness cannot put out the light, but light overcomes darkness.

You say, "But you don't know what the enemy might do!" The enemy can't do anything as long as you dwell in the light of God's Word. If you're living and walking in the light of God's Word, darkness must flee! Faith in God's Word gives you light, and that light dispels the devil's darkness.

JAMES 4:3
3   Ye ask, and receive not, because ye ask amiss, that ye may consume it upon your lusts.

Another translation says, "You ask and receive not because you ask with the wrong motives that you may consume it upon your own materialistic ways."

We need to understand that James was talking to people who were obsessed with material possessions. There is nothing wrong with material things in their proper perspective. I believe God wants to prosper His people, but I do not think that our focus should be on material possessions!

When our focus is on material things instead of on God, we get into trouble spiritually. We need to focus on what God said in His Word and on the things of God.

Acquiring material possessions is not the focus of Christianity. We are promised material goods, but they are not to be our focus. When you lose your focus in life, you lose your way and your path can get dark and muddled.

But when your life is focused on God, you know exactly what path to take in life.

> **1 TIMOTHY 6:17-19**
> **17 Charge them that are rich in this world, that they be not highminded, nor trust in uncertain riches, but in the living God, who giveth us richly all things to enjoy;**
> **18 That they do good, that they be rich in good works, ready to distribute, willing to communicate;**
> **19 Laying up in store for themselves a good foundation against the time to come, that they may lay hold on eternal life.**

Paul says that God wants to give us all good things to enjoy. So enjoying material possessions is not wrong. But desiring them above God *is* wrong. And a stingy and selfish attitude about the material possessions you have is wrong.

Seek First God's Kingdom

Jesus talked to His disciples about material things. He said if we seek God and His Kingdom first, material things will be added to us.

> **MATTHEW 6:33**
> **33 But seek ye first the kingdom of God, and his righteousness; and all these things shall be added unto you.**

Seeking God's Kingdom first is *God's* perspective on how to receive from Him. Jesus said if we seek first the Kingdom of God, material possessions would be *added* to us, not subtracted from us.

Then in another place, the Bible said, "*. . . all these blessings shall come on thee, and OVERTAKE thee, if thou shalt hearken unto the voice of the Lord thy God*" (Deut. 28:2). True prosperity comes from obeying God!

When you are busy about your Heavenly Father's business, He will take care of *your* business! But some people reverse Matthew 6:33 and seek *things* first before they seek God's Kingdom, so they don't prosper! And others give just to get, so their wrong motives hinder them from receiving from God.

I have never given an offering yet just to get something in return. There is a difference in giving just to receive and giving because you want to bless God's Kingdom. When you give to be a blessing, then you can claim God's promises and watch all these other things be added unto you!

Wrong motives make a difference with God! Even if a believer's faith is strong and he confesses God's Word, if his motives are wrong, he won't receive a return. God wants to meet the needs of His people, but sometimes He can't because their motives are all wrong!

There's a fine line between giving motivated by obedience to God's Word and giving to get something in return. When you can give with pure motives, you can expect to receive based on the promises of God. You can expect the Word to work for you. But you are not giving just to get those promises to work for you.

Your motive in giving should be to advance God's Kingdom so the gospel of the Lord Jesus Christ can be preached to the ends of the earth. That puts giving into perspective.

God doesn't want us to seek things because material possessions aren't our ultimate priority. Faith in God is a vital force in our lives, not gaining material possessions. If Jesus said they would be added to us as we seek His Kingdom—He will be faithful to keep His Word! God can't lie (Num. 23:19).

You see, some people have taken God's promises about prosperity and gotten out of balance in that area. But just because some believers have gone overboard by putting material possessions first, that doesn't mean I'm going to quit believing God!

We need to walk strong in faith, boldly proclaiming the Word. And we need to demonstrate the Word by showing what the Word produces in our lives. As we are faithful to seek God's Kingdom first, one benefit that will eventually be added to us is material blessings.

Allow God's Word to revitalize your faith! Let's rise to our full stature in Christ and proclaim, "I'm going to believe God because faith pleases God! I believe the promises in God's Word are true. We *are* who God said we are in Christ, and we *have* what God said we have in Christ. God has blessed us with all spiritual blessings in Christ!" So let's walk in the faith of God!

Chapter 6
Faith Does Not Override Free Will

And Jesus answering saith unto them, Have faith in God.

For verily I say unto you, That whosoever shall say unto this mountain, Be thou removed, and be thou cast into the sea; and shall not doubt in his heart, but shall believe that those things which he saith shall come to pass; he shall have whatsoever he saith.

Therefore I say unto you, What things soever ye desire, when ye pray, believe that ye receive them, and ye shall have them.

—Mark 11:22–24

Now faith is the substance of things hoped for, the evidence of things not seen.

—Hebrews 11:1

Let's take another look at faith! Faith—*Bible faith*—looks at negative situations and declares that God is bigger than any problem! Faith is a spiritual force that works in conjunction with other spiritual forces of God—such as love, patience, and hope—to overcome every obstacle in life.

We've looked at some common misconceptions about faith. We've seen that faith is based on God's Word. Faith doesn't mean there's an absence of a problem, and faith does not neglect natural responsibilities. And faith does not call those things that *are* as though they are *not*. In other words, faith does not ignore the problem and deny the facts. Faith "calls those things which be *not* as though they *were*" (Rom. 4:17). That's the God-kind of faith—Bible faith!

What are some other misconceptions about faith? Some believers have the idea that if they just believe God hard enough, their faith can negate the free will of others. But faith does *not* give people the ability to override the free will of others.

God gave every person free choice, and God Himself will not negate a person's free choice. We can see this principle in the Bible. God specifically said, "*You* choose whom you will serve."

If *God* won't override people's free will, we are not able to override people's free will either.

JOSHUA 24:15
15 And if it seem evil unto you to serve the Lord, choose you this day whom ye will serve; whether the gods which your fathers served that were on the other side of the flood, or the gods of the Amorites, in whose land ye dwell: but as for me and my house, we will serve the Lord.

Remember that in Mark 11:24, Jesus said, "Therefore I say unto you, whatsoever things *you* desire, when *you* pray, believe that *you* receive them, and *you* shall have them." The Bible does *not* say, "Whatsoever things you desire for *another person*, you can have what you say."

Mark 11:24 is talking about whatsoever things *you* desire that line up with the Word—not the things that someone else desires. You can't desire something for someone else unless they desire it too.

One mistake some believers make is thinking they can govern and control other people by their faith. They think if their faith is just strong enough, they can overcome another person's will. But they can't. God did not put us in charge of other people through our faith.

For example, this is true with healing. It doesn't matter how much you want someone to be healed, if that person does not want to be healed or doesn't believe it is God's will to heal him, he won't get healed—unless there is a special manifestation of the gifts of the Spirit.

We can't desire something for other people that they don't desire for themselves. God gave us faith in His Word so we could each personally receive from God. But God didn't give us faith so we could manipulate others. We can pray for others that God would show them the truths in His Word about healing, but we can't make them want to receive the healing that Jesus already provided for them.

Another area where believers have thought they could override the free will of others is in the area of marriage. For example, believers cannot believe for a certain person to be their spouse unless that person also desires it. When believers begin to believe God in some of these areas, it takes two people in agreement on the same issue to bring the petition to pass.

The Bible says, "Whatsoever things *you* desire. . . ." God didn't give us faith so we could be in dominion over other people with our faith. Now you can believe God for another person in certain areas. But by your faith, you cannot transfer your desires and your will onto someone else who does not share your desire or will.

2 CORINTHIANS 1:24
24 Not for that we have dominion over your faith, but are helpers of your joy: for by faith ye stand.

Yes, we can help others when they allow us to, but we do not have dominion over them. We can't push our desires off on others, but we can pray and intercede for them. We can witness to others by our words and by our godly lives. And we can pray and believe God for laborers to cross their paths.

For example, have you ever come across people who believe contrary to the Word of God? You'd like to talk to them about the Word, but they just don't see the truths of the Bible. Or maybe you have relatives who are not really interested in the things of God. You can't just say, "I'm going to believe God for them, and they are going to receive what God has for them—whether they want to or not!"

No, if you are praying for others to be saved, you can believe for laborers to cross their path so they can hear the Gospel. Effective laborers can influence their lives so that they begin to desire salvation, healing, and the blessings of God.

You can pray that people's hearts will be open, so they will be interested in the things of God. Once their hearts are open, the words they hear can change their mind so they can receive what God has for them.

If you know people who don't understand healing, and you can't seem to get through to them, pray and believe God to send someone across their path who can communicate to them. Pray that the eyes of their understanding will be enlightened so they can see the truth of God's Word (Eph. 1:18,19).

Then God's Word will begin to change them, so they will be able to understand the things of God. Once they begin desiring the things of God, you can hook your faith up with theirs.

But you won't be able to impose your desire on people when they have different desires than you do. God made us all free to choose our own destiny; we each have our own free volition. So if God will not violate a person's free will, why would we think we could use our faith to violate a person's free will?

God desires for everyone to be saved; He doesn't want anyone to perish. But many people are perishing because they have chosen *not* to accept God and His benefits!

Even though God desires that not one person perish, He does not come down and impose His desire and His will on people. People are free to chose Him or to reject Him. If God can't impose His will on people, then we certainly can't impose our will on others with our faith!

God made man free! Man can choose his own destiny in life—Heaven or hell. God gives man every opportunity to choose for Him. But just as God won't choose for man, you won't be able to take your faith and *make* someone choose for God either.

HOSEA 4:17
17 Ephraim is joined to idols: let him alone.

Ephraim chose to go a different direction than the one God desired for him. Finally, God said, "Let him alone." There are times when people make their own choices and until they change, nothing can be done about it.

So how do you put your faith to work for others in these situations? You pray, "Lord, bring laborers across their path who will influence them to change their desires."

That's how you exercise your faith because until people change their desires, you can't hook up with them until they come into agreement with you based on the Word of God.

When Jesus walked upon this earth, He could not change people's minds either. Remember when He stood outside of Jerusalem and wept over the city? The Israelites had rejected the way of God. Even Jesus Himself could not force His will on Jerusalem.

MATTHEW 23:37
37 O Jerusalem, Jerusalem, thou that killest the
prophets, and stonest them which are sent unto
thee, how often would I have gathered thy children together, even as a hen gathereth her chick-
ens under her wings, and ye would not!

The Israelites refused to yield to God. They refused
to turn to Him. Jesus wept over Jerusalem because He
realized what was going to happen to them because
they had rejected God.

But notice that Jesus Himself, the Son of God,
couldn't change what was going to happen to the nation
of Israel. Don't you think if Jesus could have changed
the situation, He would have? But, you see, those people living in Jerusalem had something to say about
choosing their own destiny.

This doesn't mean we should quit praying and
believing God to influence people's desires. No, we
shouldn't quit praying for people. It simply means we
must realize that we cannot override the free will of
others with our faith. Therefore, we need to know how
we *can* use our faith to help and bless people so we
don't waste our time in ineffective prayer.

For example, many people are wasting their time by
praying, "Oh, Lord, save Brother John. Save Sister
Sarah. Save Cousin Johnnie and Aunt Mary."

But God already provided for their salvation at the
Cross of Calvary! He wants them to accept their salvation. He's already done everything He can do to save
them because He gave His Son Jesus to die upon a

Cross for them. Now they have to accept the free gift of salvation that He's already provided for them.

That's why the more effective prayer is, "Lord, send laborers across their paths who will influence them for You. Send people who will help them change their desires so they want to serve You, not the enemy." That's how to use your faith effectively to pray for others.

If you know someone who says, "I don't know if it's God's will to heal me or not," begin to pray for laborers to come across that person's path. Exercise your faith for God to help him understand the Word, and then you're praying effectually.

Faith Is Not Limited to Specific Requests

I said previously that it is scriptural to have faith for specific things that God promised us in His Word. The woman with the issue of blood, blind Bartimaeus, and the crippled man at Lystra all had specific faith for the healing of their bodies. Believing God for healing is believing Him for something specific.

Therefore, we know it is scriptural to pray for specific prayer requests, because people in Jesus' day prayed specifically, and they received answers to their specific prayers. But in addition to believing God for specific requests, we also need to have a strong underlying faith that undergirds us and that we can rely upon even when everything seems to go wrong.

Yes, we can exercise our faith for specific requests, and we should because the Bible says that ". . . *all the*

promises of God in him are yea, and in him Amen . . ."
(2 Cor. 1:20). But there are also times in a believer's life
when he faces disappointments. It's during those times
when a believer can feel so far down spiritually that
he's ready to quit. But it's also during those times that
he cannot afford to throw away his faith in God.

Probably everyone has been ready to quit at some
time or another in his Christian walk. During times
like that, we need a strong underlying faith in God that
helps us determine, "No matter what happens, I still
believe God!" The Bible talks about this kind of faith in
God when everything seems to be going wrong, and we
are tempted to give up.

And during those times in life when everything
seems to go wrong, we just need to determine, "I'm
going to praise God anyway!" The Bible teaches this.

> **HABAKKUK 3:17–19**
> **17 Although the fig tree shall not blossom, neither
> shall fruit be in the vines; the labour of the olive
> shall fail, and the fields shall yield no meat; the
> flock shall be cut off from the fold, and there shall
> be no herd in the stalls:**
> **18 Yet I will rejoice in the Lord, I will joy in the
> God of my salvation.**
> **19 The Lord God is my strength, and he will make
> my feet like hinds' feet, and he will make me to
> walk upon mine high places. To the chief singer on
> my stringed instruments.**

What the Bible is saying here is that when everything goes wrong and nothing seems to be working out
right, you still need to have faith in God! Don't cast

away your confidence in Him! You need to praise Him even in the hard times, trusting that He will bring you through to victory.

For example, sometimes even members in my own congregation don't receive their healing for some reason or another. I don't always know why. Sometimes they die, and we have to preach their funerals. But I must still have a strong faith in God so that I can come back to the congregation with a determined faith that says, "I believe God regardless of circumstances or what happens to someone else!"

We just need to realize that life is not always going to be perfect as long as we live down here on this earth. We are going to face tests, trials, and temptations. But God is always going to sustain us. We just need to keep trusting Him.

You see, our faith cannot be based on everything going right all the time. Our faith shouldn't be based on whether or not we face tests, trials, or disappointments. Our faith must be based only on God's Word.

In His Word, God said He will never leave us, nor forsake us (Heb. 13:5). So it doesn't matter what circumstances look like or what it seems like in the natural, we must still have that strong undergirding faith that declares, "Here I am and here I stand, live or die, sink or swim, go under or go over—I stand with God!"

God said, "Heaven and earth will pass away, but My Word will never pass away" (Matt. 24:35). Therefore, I am going to walk with God regardless of circumstances. I'm going to walk according to His Word. I'm not going to allow circumstances to shake my faith—even when I pray for someone and the person doesn't get healed.

People ask me all the time, "Don't you get upset when people don't get healed?"

Yes, it bothers me when people don't get healed because I have such a desire and a compassion to see them healed. But I'm not going to quit praying for the sick just because some people don't get healed!

A couple of years ago, I preached the funeral for one of our traveling ministers. That was difficult. At times like that, it would have been easy to quit preaching that God heals. But God is still God. And the Word is still the Word. And faith in God still works.

People ask, "Why wasn't that young man healed?"

I don't know! But I do know this. If you allow the enemy to torment you to continually ask, "Why? Why? Why?" every time you hit a crisis, you will never advance any further spiritually.

In fact, the enemy can cause you to get discouraged and turn back if you are always questioning why things happen. The question you should ask yourself is not "Why?" but "Do I still trust God in spite of the fact that I don't understand everything that happens in life?"

People come to me all the time saying, "But I just don't understand!" Then they try to make sense of some circumstance in their life, but finally they just sort of sputter to a stop. They think maybe I have the answer as to why a particular thing happened in their life as it did.

I look at them and I say, "I don't understand either, but God is still in the healing business. He is still in the

saving business, and He is still in the delivering business. And whether or not I understand every negative
circumstance, I still believe God!"

Our faith in God shouldn't be grounded on understanding everything that happens to us in life. Genuine
faith in God determines to believe God's Word regardless of negative situations.

"But," someone said, "I knew So-and-so, and I know
she was believing God for her healing. You can't tell me
she wasn't! So why did she die?" Even though I may
not have every answer, I do know one thing: God is still
God. And the Word is still the Word!

I also know this: Your faith needs to be so rooted
and grounded in God's Word that regardless of circumstances, you can face setbacks, disappointment, or
adversity and declare, "No matter what happens, I
believe God!" That's strong, mature faith.

Strong Faith in God

The great man of faith, the Apostle Paul, demonstrated his strong determined faith when he said that
in spite of all the trials and tribulations that confronted
him, nothing could separate him from the love of God.

> ROMANS 8:35,37–39
> 35 Who shall separate us from the love of Christ?
> shall tribulation, or distress, or persecution, or
> famine, or nakedness, or peril, or sword? . . .
> 37 Nay, in all these things we are more than con-
> querors through him that loved us.
> 38 For I am persuaded, that neither death, nor

**life, nor angels, nor principalities, nor powers, nor
things present, nor things to come,
39 Nor height, nor depth, nor any other creature,
shall be able to separate us from the love of God,
which is in Christ Jesus our Lord.**

Paul demonstrated his strong faith in God when he
didn't waver in spite of all the tribulations he suffered:
he was left for dead, beaten, shipwrecked, bitten by a
viper, escaped from a city at night. He demonstrated his
strong faith in God by counting his suffering as nothing
compared to serving Jesus.

PHILIPPIANS 3:8
**8   Yea doubtless, and I count all things but loss
for the excellency of the knowledge of Christ
Jesus my Lord: for whom I have suffered the loss
of all things, and do count them but dung, that I
may win Christ.**

Sometimes believers try to use faith without wisdom. But it's best to use faith *and* wisdom together.
That's what the Apostle Paul did when the Apostles let
him down from the city wall so he could escape!

ACTS 9:22–25
**22 But Saul increased the more in strength, and
confounded the Jews which dwelt at Damascus,
proving that this is very Christ.
23 And after that many days were fulfilled, the
Jews took counsel to kill him:
24 But their laying await was known of Saul. And
they watched the gates day and night to kill him.
25 Then the disciples took him by night, and let
him down by the wall in a basket.**

If Paul had been like some faith people I know today, they never would have lived to preach another sermon. They would have tried to keep on preaching, saying, "Bless God, by faith, I'm going to preach!" They may have used their faith, but without using any wisdom!

And even though their life was in danger, they would have kept on preaching, and it may have cost them their life.

But even in spite of all of Paul's sufferings and peril, he wrote, "Nothing can separate us from the love of God." In spite of beatings, imprisonment, and sufferings, Paul declared, "I'm more than a victor." No matter what happened in life, Paul's faith was in Jesus Christ.

For example, even though he had to slip out of the city under the cover of darkness, Paul still declared, "I thank my God, I always triumph in Christ Jesus. I am a victor because I am more than a conqueror in Him who loves me!"

Faith Is Not the Absence of Feeling

Many believers think that when they are standing strong in faith, they will not experience feelings. They think faith negates feelings.

And it is true, the Bible says, *"For we walk by faith, not by sight"* (2 Cor. 5:7). We could say it this way: "The just walk by *faith*, not by *feelings*." This statement is vital to strong faith because feelings fluctuate and can't always be depended upon. We can't measure truth by feelings. We can only measure truth by what God's Word says because it is the only eternal *fact*.

But at the same time, we must realize that God gave us emotions and feelings. Although they were never meant to govern us, emotions are still beneficial. We can have strong faith and still experience feelings. Faith is not the absence of feeling. It's just that we can't walk by our feelings when they contradict God's Word.

However, the way some people talk, they give the impression that God wants us to be unemotional like robots. They think it's wrong if we even mention the word "feelings." Some believers even criticize others for saying, "I feel good!"

I've had believers tell me, "Feelings don't have anything to do with it, brother!"

Well, I don't know about you, but I'd rather feel good than bad. I've been in both camps and feeling good is better!

We can have feelings! We just need to understand that feelings don't necessarily have anything to do with what we believe. The Bible determines what we believe, not our feelings.

But even Jesus Christ experienced feelings as He walked upon this earth. Do you believe Jesus was a spiritual faith person when He walked on this earth? Well, He experienced the full spectrum of emotions. Read the New Testament!

For example, we can see that Jesus wept at Lazarus' tomb (John 11:35). At times, Jesus was angry. Some people say, "Jesus could never be angry!" Well, why do you think He picked up a whip and ran those money changers out of the temple! He was righteously indignant because they were disgracing His Father's house.

JOHN 2:13–16
13 And the Jews' passover was at hand, and Jesus went up to Jerusalem.
14 And found in the temple those that sold oxen and sheep and doves, and the changers of money sitting:
15 And when he had made a scourge of small cords, he drove them all out of the temple, and the sheep, and the oxen; and poured out the changers' money, and overthrew the tables;
16 And said unto them that sold doves, Take these things hence; make not my Father's house an house of merchandise.

Jesus was righteously indignant! The Bible says that Jesus even turned tables over, and drove the merchants out of the temple with a whip. He didn't just *suggest* that they leave the temple or nonchalantly *ask* them to leave. The Bible said He *drove* them out.

Well, if you've ever seen cowhands drive a herd of cattle on the open range, you know that when they want to get those cattle moving, they don't do it nonchalantly! They crack that whip!

The Apostle Paul was also a great man of faith, but he expressed emotion and feelings in much of his writing. For example, Epaphroditus, one of the young men of his spiritual company almost died, and Paul's feelings about that incident came out in his writings.

PHILIPPIANS 2:27
27 For indeed he [Epaphroditus] was sick nigh unto death: but God had mercy on him; and not on him only, but on me also, lest I should have sorrow upon sorrow.

Paul said that if Epaphroditus had died, Paul would have had sorrow upon sorrow. That's emotion! Sorrow is a feeling. Therefore, Paul experienced some sorrow when his helper and friend Epaphroditus was sick.

So here is a man who wrote more about faith than anyone else in the Bible, and he's talking about feelings! Many people say we are not supposed to experience any feelings. But that can put the Body of Christ into bondage because that makes it difficult to work through some situations if believers always feel condemned for experiencing emotions.

Just because you are a faith person does not negate the fact that you also are an emotional person! Our emotions are not supposed to govern our faith, but it's not wrong to experience some feelings and emotions.

Some people have even said that believers shouldn't weep or feel sorrow when a loved one dies. Sorrow is usually accompanied by tears and a feeling of loneliness and despair. But Paul himself said that if Epaphroditus had died, he would have had sorrow upon sorrow. But the Bible doesn't say that we are not to sorrow or cry when someone dies. It just says that we are not to sorrow as the world sorrows.

1 THESSALONIANS 4:13
13 . . . sorrow not, even as others which have no hope.

The Bible doesn't say not to have sorrow. It just said, "Don't be like those who sorrow with no hope." It doesn't say, "Don't shed tears." It only says not to be like those who shed tears with no hope. There is a big difference between shedding tears because you are going to miss someone who's gone to be with the Lord, and the grief the world feels when their loved ones die, because they have no hope of eternal life!

The Greater One Will Strengthen You!

Here is another principle we need to understand. Even though you experience emotions, you can begin to release your faith by drawing strength from the Greater One on the inside of you. The Holy Spirit within will help stabilize you in times of sorrow or grief!

Actually, emotions can act as a warning, alerting you to the fact that you need to get in faith! In other words, sometimes you wouldn't even realize you're in trouble unless your negative emotions alerted you to that fact.

Once your feelings alert you that you are not in faith, begin to grab hold of the promises of God. For example, when you're feeling afraid and anxious, you know you need to renew your mind with the Word so you can get in faith about the situation!

You don't go around hollering, "Lord, thank You for healing me" when you don't have any symptoms. Many times, it's only when you get in touch with your feelings in the physical realm that you realize you are having problems! Then you can begin to put your faith out for that situation.

When you begin to feel emotions of sorrow, despair, and depression, it should alert you to turn to the

Greater One on the inside who is there to comfort and strengthen you.

You see, it's not wrong to have feelings and emotions! Jesus had emotions. Paul had emotions. If you've ever read the Psalms of David, you realize that David expressed quite a variety of emotions, including anger, despair, and disappointment.

But at the same time, notice that David always turned and immediately began to declare the greatness of God. For example, when Saul was chasing David and his men all over the country, David declared, "God is my fortress! He is my refuge and my strong tower!"

So don't feel condemned if you experience emotions. Even the great patriarchs of old experienced emotions, but they still lived for God and experienced great triumphs in their lives!

Many believers today condemn others for their feelings and emotions. They'll tell others, "Oh, brother, don't talk about feelings! Feelings don't have anything to do with faith!"

It's true that feelings don't have anything to do with believing God. In other words, we base our faith on His Word, not on how we feel. But we do have feelings. We just don't base our faith on our emotions. If we do, we're going to be in trouble. Faith in God definitely helps us deal and work through these feelings and emotions, but faith does not imply the absence of emotion.

Strong faith is not the absence of strong feelings and emotions. You can have strong faith and still experience feelings and emotions. When you are in faith, you just don't allow your feelings to govern you. The Word of God is to govern us in all the affairs of life. When you put the Word first, your feelings must come subject to the Word of God.

Real faith in God—Bible faith—is much different than many people have thought. Faith in God does not insulate you from encountering life's problems, but it does ensure that you come out of every situation as the victor, not the victim! Also, faith does not deny circumstances, nor does it deny the facts. But armed with the greater facts of God's Word, the believer who is in faith can overcome any circumstance because God's Word never fails!